The Diary of Jasmine Grace

Jasmine Grace Marino

DEDICATION

This book is dedicated to the countless women and girls—and even the boys and men—who don't know that there is a better way. To those who are still out there sick and suffering, you desperately need to know that Hope is alive and waiting for you. To my own children, I trust that you will never experience what I did. May you always feel loved, cherished and worthy—no matter what.

ACKNOWLEDGMENTS

First and foremost, I have to thank my God and Savior, Jesus! Where would I be without Your saving grace? To Keith, I love you for many reasons, especially because you see me for who I am today and not who I was. To my parents, for always leaving the door open when I had nowhere else to go. To both of my grandmothers Nonnie Lil and Nonnie Ellie, for always loving and believing in me. To all my friends who I've met along the messy journey of my recovery, your unconditional love and support has propelled me into this space of healing and writing.

I want to thank Bonnie Gatchell, founder and director of Route One Ministry. Because of you, my friend, I was able to identify as a survivor of sex trafficking. Here's a BIG shout out to Lisa Goldblatt Grace and Audrey Morrissey from My Life My Choice in Boston, MA. You both helped me find my voice when you hired me to be a survivor mentor and join the anti-trafficking movement. To mentor, friend and survivor leader Rebecca Bender, you have inspired me to mature and continue fighting the good fight. I have to thank my counselor Kristen Kansiewicz, because you showed me what it means to be a godly woman.

A great big thank you goes to all those who financially supported my ministry work through the Emmanuel Gospel Center in Boston. This writing and self-publishing wouldn't have happened without your faithful and generous giving during the past three years. To Sarah Dunham and others at EGC, thank you for giving me a place to learn, grow and do the work I've been called to do.

Thank you, Rachael Smith, for all the work you did on the cover. Jodi Hyer, I appreciate the many hours you spent reading and checking this raw material. Your friendship means the world to me. To Rosie Clandos, science writer and editor, thank you for teaching me to improve this craft of writing. You are a godsend.

Lastly, I want to thank all the survivors who I have met over the years. You have given me the courage to continue sharing my story *because I knew I wasn't the only one.*

Trafficking

According to the U.S. Department of Justice, "The term 'human trafficking' is used in common parlance to describe many forms of exploitation of human beings. While these words often evoke images of undocumented migrants being smuggled across international borders, the term has a different and highly specific meaning under the United States Criminal Code. Human trafficking crimes, which are defined in Title 18, Chapter 77, focus on the act of compelling or coercing a person's labor, services, or commercial sex acts. The coercion can be subtle or overt, physical or psychological, but it must be used to coerce a victim into performing labor, services, or commercial sex acts. Because these statutes are rooted in the prohibition against slavery and involuntary servitude guaranteed by the Thirteenth Amendment to the United States Constitution, the Civil Rights Division plays a paramount role in enforcing these statutes, alongside our partners in the United States Attorneys' offices (USAOs) and law enforcement agencies."

https://www.justice.gov/crt/human-trafficking-prosecution-unit-htpu
Retrieved on December 13, 2016.

"Therefore, if the Son makes you free,
you shall be free indeed."
John 8:36

Jasmine Grace

CHAPTERS

PREFACE

Just an ordinary girl.

I was 18 years old. I just graduated from a vocational high school and passed the test in front of the cosmetology board. I was excited to be a licensed hairdresser, but I was also attending a community college and majoring in journalism to achieve my long-term goal of becoming a writer. I dreamed of maybe moving to New York someday to write for one of those big name magazines. But my dreams quickly faded as I got involved with a guy I met at a local night club.

It was a regular Friday or Saturday night. My girls and I were already drunk before we entered the club with our fake I.D's. We were having a good time, dancing and pushing away any whack-ass dudes that tried to step up to us. Then this guy walked up. He knew one of my friend's boyfriends so he was automatically cool. He was a good-looking African-American in his early twenties. I'll call him Brian or B.

He brought me to the bar and offered to buy me a drink. When he pulled out a stack of money with his blinged-out bracelet dripping in diamonds and gold, he had my full attention. I did the once over, following the shine up to his ears and then to the necklace with the Jesus piece and thought: "Hmm, this dude might be worth my time."

He was an ugrade. I had never dated a guy who looked so successful. Being wanted or liked by someone who had riches and power made me feel like I had succeeded.

You should know that I had just been dumped by a guy that I was dating off and on for almost two years, and recently I had an abortion. He already had two children; he said I was too young and not ready to have his kid. I was broken, naive and looking for someone to love me—maybe even fix or save me.

B and I exchanged phone numbers, and we began to chat over the phone. After a few weeks, we met up to chill in East Boston. I lived a few towns over, but most of my friends lived in Eastie, and he was working as a registry runner for one of the car dealerships nearby. He pulled up in his champagne-colored Mercedes Benz. I got in and saw that his eyes were hazy from smoking weed. He was cool, calm and full of compliments. Right away he started to tell me about his registry business—how he was an entrepreneur and was "all about making that money". He asked me questions about my life. We were getting to know each other.

After that night, we started to hang out often. He would take me out and buy me fancy clothes and shoes. I felt special and began trusting him because he was paying so much attention to me. I learned he grew up around crime, drugs and violence in the inner city of Boston. He never knew his father and said his mother raised him and two other siblings. B was the hustler of the family and took care of his mother, even though she worked. They managed to get out of the ghetto and move to a better area just outside of Boston.

I confided in him and told him that I wanted to be a writer. He would say things like: "Why would you want to write for a magazine when you could own it?" or "Why would you want to work in a salon? I can see you owning the salon and just doing hair for fun." These statements were way out of my league. How was a young girl like me ever going to own anything? I was only 19 at this time. He was trying to build confidence in me and have me see him as the guy who I would have to stay loyal to. He was saying he could help make all these dreams come true.

He just didn't say how.

One night, I was invited by a guy friend to a party at a state college. I walked into a small apartment to find a bunch of drunken college guys. I was expecting a good time—to hang out and get drunk—when the unthinkable happened. My friend told me that the entertainment was coming. He hired a dancer from an agency. I didn't think anything of it until the girl walked in, and she was my best friend, Suzanne! I was in complete shock because I hadn't seen her in a while. I knew she had moved in with a new boyfriend, but I didn't know that she became a stripper!!

As I began to cry, she was utterly embarrassed. And, yes, I ruined the party. She left. I drank myself into oblivion.

Weeks later, I told B about that situation. He told me that he happened to know Suzanne's man and asked if I wanted to talk to her. I jumped at the opportunity to call her. When we got on the phone, we were both excited and happy to talk. I apologized for ruining her dancing gig at the college. She let me know that's what she had been doing since she got down with her new man. She mentioned that she was living in a big house with some other girls who she called her "wives-in-law", and I should visit.

B took me to Suzanne's house. I was impressed with the Range Rover and BMW in the driveway. The house was in the expensive area of Boston and had a fence around it for privacy. Suzanne had her own bedroom with lots of clothes, shoes and jewelry.

She convinced me that her life was amazing. She probably believed that because when a girl is new to the life of prostitution, she tells herself that—just to get through the day. As we caught up, she told me that she worked in a massage parlor in Maine where she made up to $1,000 a day turning tricks. She had to give it all to her man, but she said he provided all she needed. So, in her mind, it wasn't a bad deal because he was promising her the good life.

She taught me how to service the johns and what to say to them so they would give me more money. I left from her house that day, wondering if this life was going to work out for me.

And that, my friend, is how the grooming process of pimping and prostitution works. The pimp spots the vulnerable girl who lacks self-worth and is looking for validation, so he can easily make her feel loved, safe and special. Then she falls in love with him. When he asks her to sell her body to complete strangers, she's not thrilled with the idea, but she wants him to continue loving her. It's a form of brainwashing, manipulation and control. It gets worse, and it doesn't end like a fairy-tale. Every girl has a different story, but the process is the same.

This is just the beginning of my story: The Diary of Jasmine Grace.

From here I'll take you on my journey, through the pages of my journal that I kept as I was being exploited in the life by my boyfriend who turned pimp/trafficker.

Miraculously this journal survived all these turbulent and traumatic times, just as I have. I'll share some of my daily entries that capture the manipulation, abuse and fear that kept me under his control for five years and during the cycle of exploitation and addiction that came afterward. After each journal entry, I've written my thoughts as a healed and whole survivor looking back at the brokenness of my life in prostitution.

Throughout this book, names have been changed.

Chapter 1

Diary: Year 2000

May 25, 2000

Well today is a beautiful sunny day. It has been raining for a couple days so It's good to finally see the sun. Well school is out for the summer and I am excited, now I can just chill, go 2 the gym & work without worrying about homework! (yip-yee) I'm just waiting to get my report card, which I know will be good :)

Well me and B are doing our thing - I've been doing a lot of thinking and testing the waters & wondering why life is so weird! Do we control our own fate? Or is fate just destiny? B & I are getting down with business, money & stuff. Suzanne and I talk on the reg about things, her life, mines & how to handle shit.

Life is changing. It's all about the fittest, survival, sacrifices, decisions and being the flossiest. Gotta get that Bling Bling!! No - but really life comes & goes fast, we can only live once, so like Nike, should I just DO IT? Get in the game? Well the decision is this, Yes I will, for myself, the experience, B & the money that can be made.

I am writting now, that I will not get greedy, or let the money go to my head. I will just see how this works & be smart. Be on my toes at all times & know my surroundings. B made a good point when he said "Jazz, tomorrow isn't promised, so live for today." And ya know - he made sense. Everyday I'll wake up & be thankful, God is giving me another day of breath.

So change has arrived, moving on, getting a little older, learning a little more everyday. I really don't think this life, is the one for me, but hey for a little while it will be good. I could lavish for a couple! & if I die tommorow (God forbid) then hey, look at what I've accomplished till now. So I'll c-ya later. Keep Strong!

September 18, 2014

New Door

As I look back at that young girl, I feel sad that she was so lost. She had a big choice in front of her, but because of fears, doubts and insecurities she walked through the wrong door, a door that would change her life forever.

As I opened up the journal today, a quote fell out that I had cut from the newspaper back then, and I thought it was very fitting for this reflection: "Sometimes entering a new door can make a great change in one's life." Just as I walked through the wrong door back then, I am willingly walking through another door today. I am choosing to look back and move forward to use my pain for someone else's healing. Only this time, I can see the light.

June 18, 2000

Well today is a peaceful day. I haven't gotten hardly any sleep the past week. But I'll be ok. I called into Great Cuts this morning. Last night B, Jake, Maria & I stayed at hotel. It was ok but some drama cuz Jake is just like that. But otherwise it's cool. I started working @ the net, 3Gs* in 2 weeks which is awesome!

B & I are really working things out, we are doing good. We think a like, we act a like, we are on the same page. Most of the time. Yes *he's my man. My P*. He understands me a lot & respects what I am thinking or my opion, whatever opinion. It's different or the same as his. He's cool & as long as he keeps it real, then he is my numero uno 4 life! For real, there is a major connection & we go good together!*

Now on the other hand, Jake & Maria are getting along but personally, i think he is rushing things. I mean Maria is still a little young. She has a little more growing up to do & i really don't want J to push her. I'd feel really bad if things didn't work out cuz she's a good kid. But oh well, ya live & learn. right.

So anyways I'm sitting here on my hammock, just chillin, breathing, meditating, living life. Thinking about stuff, & how i can make life better. Great Cuts will be history on June 22. I'll miss everyone but then again I'll get over it. I'm getting sleepy just swinging back & forth. I think I'll stop writting, my minds seems pretty clear. C-ya - now that I've kept strong through this change, I gotta Stay strong. Peace.

*3Gs = $3,000

*My P = my pimp

September 25, 2014

Connecticut

The "net" was a nasty, dark and dirty massage parlor in Hartford, Connecticut. I was sent there first because my pimp knew it was difficult. The tips were cheap; the men were gross and could be violent. It had a reputation for being like the street, except indoors. I worked 10:00 a.m. to 1:00 a.m. (15 hours!) and slept in a nearby motel. I was there for three to four days in a row. B knew it was only a matter of time before I would have to quit the hair salon. He was slowly isolating me from any type of normal life, and he knew I would become addicted to making lots of money.

July 11, 2000

I am doin Ok. I almost said Bye-Bye to B for life, but then we worked out our problems. It wasn't easy. This hole change thing, getting settled & used to working isn't as easy as I thought it would be. But B & I are working hard to make this right & I know we will pull through this hard time, at the begining! :)

I hope, cuz I'm really feeling B. I mean he is the Best, My match, I found him, the only problem is that he wants to be my P & I want him to be a regular dude, who will love me & want to be with just me one day. Cuz I see B & B shouldn't be in this game, he's too real, he has too much love, & life in him to be a P. He is better than that, So I will make the scarifice for him, & he will make the sacrafice for me. No other chics, right now & 4 awhile, we need a crib & our shit settled first, my mental also needs to be ready. I almost love this kid! Soul mate? Can you say that, I found that? I found the most compatable man on earth, when I think of him a smile comes across my face, & I picture him, it makes me feel good. But I really want to know if the same happens to him? :) I wish.

Well anyways things are Ok. I'm alive, breathing & full of life. Maria and Jake are no more & I knew that was gonna happen. Well gotta go. C-ya

October 2, 2014

Love

Falling in love with a man who does not love you and does not intend to love you, is a heartbreaking reality. Wishing B would love me propelled me into an unhealthy space of "working harder and sacrificing more" to get that love from him. It never happened. In my recovery, I have experienced true unconditional love through my growing relationship with God. Jesus Christ sacrificially died on a cross, so I wouldn't have to work so hard to ear love. That simple message is

the reason I share my story with others. Oh, so they would know that love, too.

July 14, 2000

Well what a day, can B & I work this out? I'm in love with a pimp. Hello. What did I fall into? B won't drop the hole game but he will sacrifice for me - no other chics. Just me & him but I hate the fact that in order to be with him I have work and on top of that, pay the dude.! I feel like I am buyin him, what type of relationship is that, ya he won't be a full fledged pimp but he'll still be getting paid by me!

I don't understand him at all. I wish he could just give it up. Yo forget about it. When we fought all day yesterday he got so violent & I got so emotional. It was terrible, I can't believe I finally find a dude that's real, so real it seems fake, so real, I get nervous like, Whoa, where did this dude come from? but he can be mines? Wow but he can only be mines for a price & that price is whatever I sell my self for. Now is that really worth it? Does this dude mean that much to me, that I will put my self for sale, just so we can get paid?

He says it's for us, but ya know something, I don't need the money that bad. I'll miss him for sure. I'll always remember him but for real. I don't need it. I need someone to love me for me. Not cuz I'm bringing some money to the table. Why can't he just be my man, a regular dude - I mean we have so much fun together, he's the best, like my best friend, boyfriend with benefits! How much better can you get that B and I. If you can then it's worth a mil cuz me & B are priceless. ain't no one like us. To bad he wants to be pimp daddy for a while. He could have been a great boyfriend. Friend or whatever someone like him could share everything with. Give anything to him.

But going against what I believe in, I tried it. Tried to do it. And it keeps comin back to me. Like Jazz - Hello, girl this isn't for you. You have a conscience. You care about yourself & my mental health is going down the drain, messing with this dude - first I know he's good. I got a good vibe, so I stick around then I try to fool myself & go be a ho. Then I fall in love with him cuz I'm with him all the time & I start to see him - clearly, the realist dude, I've ever come across, now I want him all to myself. Cuz he is the best. So no other chics. Ok. Then I can't pay him, why cuz I like him & I want him to like me back. Regardless of money, cuz I like him...

And he ain't doing shit for me, except being there - literally. Just there. Being B. Being real. If I'm in the net, then I gotta come out of each session with no less than $100. Wow, what kind of sick shit is that? - I can't handle that shit. I'm setteling for less being with him. There will be another dude out there for me & ya know what after this tramitizing shit, I really don't give a shit about any other dudes, just myself, because myself is what is always gonna be there for me. no-one else. So B - it was real. Love ya C-ya.

October 9, 2014

Reality

I was confused. I was being pulled into a life of darkness and pain. The promise of love was what I was searching for and desperately needed. A common tactic that many traffickers use is to lure young girls and women by promising to be a loving boyfriend.

B wasn't being totally honest with me. He was selling a fake dream by manipulating me. He had found my vulnerability—my need and desire to be loved and accepted. Looking me in the eyes, promising to keep it real by being upfront with his feelings, and telling me about the rules for the game made me feel secure in the relationship. The reality is that it was total deception. He told me that he loved me, but being a pimp was the way he had to make money. When I would ask, how long we would have to do it, he would promise, "not long". Also, he said that he would be willing to sacrifice for me and not have any other girls work for him. One of the comments he often said was, "Love don't pay the bills, so get your ass to work." I would feel guilty for not reciprocating. I thought he

was bending the rules of the game by not having other women, because I thought he really loved me.

July 30, 2000

Well, life is full of surprises & unexpected things. Well, I'm still in the net. I never left. Well, I took a little vacation (like a week) & now I'm trying to write how I felt when I decided to write. But, I read what I wrote last time so now I feel like a weirdo - like I can't make up my mind. So, I feel stupid cuz my feelings are changed once again.

B and I bought a couch & TV. They are both on layaway. Ok, so now my mind is somewhat straight: It's a money thing. Period. Yeah, I like B. I like B a alot. So ok I found someone that I like & is really cool. So let's make money. I feel better when he does his hustle cuz then he's not all depending on me. I like that cuz I don't need no more dudes depending on me for shit.

So I realized that B & I can do things and progess! So now, my feelings are switched, Yes I love him? (love what a strong word). But I've learned how to kinda separate business and pleasure. We can do this. We are looking for a crib and for some reason, I feel like he's procrastinating. Like he really don't want to. Last month dude spent my $5G's - Wow - & he wants me to trust him w/ all this. Yo, I'm trying to fall back* but it's hard cuz I'm not in total control, like I'm used to.

So, Ok. The job is somewhat easy - the money is good - So let's do it. Fuck it, yo. Make money, maybe. Hopefully open a phat* salon. Still go to school but for business, get a degree. B - just look at him like I did all the other dudes. Fuck it. He does whatever he does and I keep an eye on that. But always remember who I am. And watch my surroundings. At. All. Times.

I definitely stopped the intense feelings I had for him cuz it wasn't working. I was falling for him. Some serious shit. So No More. I'll stay right where I am w/ my feelings. No further. No Less. I just gotta remember to love myself.

Cherish your yesterdays, Dream your tomorrows & Live your todays.

Bye.

*Phat = really nice, expensive things

*Fall back = back off, lay low

October 16, 2014

Love and Money

I was fighting with myself on paper. Can you see my racing thoughts?

I knew it was wrong to love a pimp; but for the first time, I had a man in my life who was doing everything he could to get me to love and trust him. I knew it wasn't true love. I knew I had to keep up my guard, so I fought back the feelings and tried to keep it "just business". I remember a very vivid dream I had around that same time. When I called my friend and gave her the details, she looked it up in a dream interpretation book. The meaning was that I was being influenced by the wrong people, and the person talking to me in the dream was concerned for me. I don't know how reliable dream books are, but the question remains: What if I had taken heed to that warning?

Making five thousand dollars in a few weeks is very addicting and can become a problem for anyone. Fast money gave me a false sense of power, control and security—even though I was never in need of material things when I was growing up because my parents provided for me.

My concern is for the girl who comes out of poverty or a low-income environment. Making all that money is like winning the lottery. The problem is that she will never get to spend it or save it in the way she desires. This has been a difficult area for me in my recovery because I had to learn how to live on a budget and a minimum-wage salary. Yes, I said BUDGET. I never knew what that was until I had bills to pay and no more money under my mattress! Financial stress plays a huge role in why so many women go back into the life of prostitution. Often, it is the only way they know how to survive.

Snapshot of the records I kept, tracking the amount of money I earned. I wasn't allowed to keep any of it for myself.

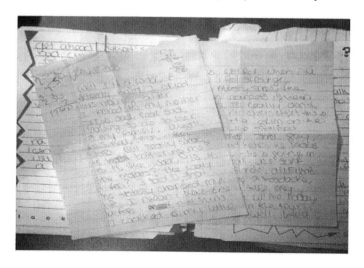

Photo of my actual diary pages.

July 31, 2000

Well I'm @ work & extremly bored. I cried this morning after I talked to my mother. It's sad, real sad. Having to lie to her & my family. B feels bad that I feel bad. But really what is bothering me? Is it the work. Is it the morals? The way I feel? I told B that he totally changed my life. I mean I was fine before I met him. I worked @ my little Great Cuts, made my little money & was content. B came into my life and I was blinded. I like him so much that it didn't really matter about leaving my job or my "normal" life. I figured everything would work out & ya know - it really isn't working anymore.

I feel confused & kinda alone but I don't know why. I miss my Ma, I miss my home, I miss my work when I think about it. I keep on getting interrupted, these girls are talking to me. It's weird when I'm here I feel strange. The musty smell, the green carpets, green doors. I really don't think, I'll ever 4-get this place. The grime on the walls, the stained mattresses. Some guy just said hello, he looks familiar - he's going in with Crystal. The soft spoken blonde.

Alright I'm getting a headache. I 4-got to take my medication with me today. I left it in the trunk. OOps. - Oh Well. Well my break is coming. If I feel like I gotta write, I will later. I think I really miss home and B. I wanna go home. I'm tired, hungry and just fed up.:(

October 23, 2014

New Identity

This journal entry has been the most difficult to write so far. As I re-read this entry it takes me right back to that grimy massage parlor. I remember the smell and feel of the place like it was yesterday even though it has been over 14 years ago. Even the paper I wrote on looks dirty. I don't want to touch it. I feel like going to wash my hands right now.

Dirty and confused is how I felt on a daily basis. I would scrub my body after each session and again at the end of the night, just to get that feeling to go away. Lying to my mother was horrible and also produced more shame inside of me.

24

Everything about my life was a lie.

They even changed my name. Tami was my new identity. I was becoming someone I didn't want to be from 11:00 a.m. until 1:00 a.m. four days a week. On the other days, I was B's "bottom bitch"—the one he claimed to love and want to be with. I had to "hold it down" for him and make him proud by making a lot of money.

I am so grateful for my new identity today. I have been truly washed clean. I know that I am a beloved daughter of the Most High King. I am a Princess Warrior fighting the battle for the many women and girls who are out there right now— trapped, lonely and afraid.

In 2008, when I was new to the faith, I found this verse in the Bible very comforting. I love that I can still go to it today, especially in this moment and remember the truth about who I am.

"Come now, and let us reason together," says the Lord. "Though your sins are like scarlet, they shall be as white as snow; though they are red like crimson, they shall be as wool." Isaiah 1:18

August 8, 2000

Well today is another day.. My life keeps on changing. One minute I'm happy. The next minute I'm depressed. I'm calling out to B, but he just can't hear me. I feel terrible. Doing what I'm doing isn't right. Why am I going to work & then coming home and giving my all to B? I never really thought it was right, but I did it - So no more. 4-get it. I need time to think, time away. To myself.

B says that I'm scared that I don't want to be with him cuz I'm afraid it's gonna be to good. Cuz I mean, yeah B & I are dangerous. Yes we're the best. I've never connected with someone like I connect with B. Never ever before could I find someone so compatable.

I really like him & that's another reason why I can't do this. Why must I work, in order for him to be with me? That's sad. I want B to love me be with me whether I'm broke, rich - whatever. This will never happen. B will never be my regular boyfriend. I will scream this out 4-ever & he will never understand me. Cuz he says this is the only way we can get ahead. That's to bad cuz I really feel for him. But I can't hold on to something that's not there. So I'm gonna write him a letter. Maybe he'll understand me better that way.

I'll miss him.

Na, I can't write him a letter.

October 28, 2014

Vacate

I did take time away. I went on a one-week vacation with my mother to Miami Beach, Florida, and I talked with him on the phone for most of the time. He would call me and tell me how much he missed me and to come home to Daddy. Nothing I said mattered because he wasn't interested in hearing me. All he wanted to do was silence me and make money off of my body. He did this by being really nice, changing the subject or making me laugh.

Sometimes he would use violence. The first time he got violent was in the car when we were driving home from Hartford. As I was driving, I said something he didn't like. He backhanded me so hard that the side of my head hit the window. I had to pull over because my vision became blurry, and I couldn't see the road. He pulled me out of the car and proceeded to beat me on the side of the highway until the other pimp that was in the backseat pulled him off of me. They threw me in the backseat, and I cried the entire way home, wondering how I got myself into this situation and how was I going to get out.

August 30, 2000

Well my birthday was good. Maria, Suzanne and I went to the club. We had a good time! Wow I can't believe I'm 20. Whoa! Now that I'm 20, I have to get a plan & stick to it. I went back with B. But once again it didn't work. I went to Maine today just to observe - but nope! Came home and changed my cell phone number! Cuz B & I got into a fight over the STD we have. Yes it's probably my fault. But when I found out I told B and he didn't take care of it so I got it back.

Bottom line is that I don't trust him. I just can't. When I call his house they tell me he's not there, then he calls me and he say's he's home! Hello! Staying over other girls houses! Staying over Lacy's house?? What kind of shit is that? Having mad other girls #s in his pockets. Then getting mad when I ask him?!

And the violence really bothers me. He's hit me numerous times & I've still stayed around! I'm sick, stressed, depressed & fed up. I'm not settling for this shit anymore. He fucked with me way tooooo much now.

I will get back on my own two feet & live my life the way I want to live it. Take care of myself, cuz that's the only way I will get treated right. I'll think of him often & miss him. (I'm starting to cry) :(but I will survive. I'll get over it. i feel bad but not hopeless. Never will I feel like nothing with out B, or anyone for that matter.

god please help me through this, give me that strength i need. please. Just as bad as I don't want to talk to him i wish he would call. But oh well, he don't love me. So c-ya. Get out of my life just as quick as you came in. Bye. <3 Jazz

*A goal: where do I want to be in 5 years? in another state, living my life to the fullest, working at a salon, doing hair, traveling and seeing the world! * Come on Jazz - get it 2-gether.

October 30, 2014

Attempted Freedom

This entry is just scratching the surface of my journey into darkness. If you stay with the story and keep reading long enough, you will see me disappear.

The game of pimping is like domestic violence on steroids. The amount of shame a woman feels is beyond words when forced prostitution gets added to an unhealthy, violent relationship. Not only was I getting STDs, beaten, manipulated and lied to, but also I had to sell my body in order to receive love from this man. Can you understand the dynamics of power and control? The entry tells a story of hope and fear. I really wanted to leave him and make a life for myself, but I couldn't break free. By confusing me, he was controlling my mind and my body.

Lacy was another girl he had who was selling drugs for him on the side. He tried to keep Lacy and me separate. I was jealous of her because she was around before me, and I knew she loved him, too. He claimed they were just business partners.

At the same time, there was talk about another massage parlor in Kittery, Maine. I was complaining so badly about working in Hartford that Maine seemed promising. It was more upscale and expensive. He knew he would make more money with me working in Maine, and there were some benefits for me. My friend Suzanne was working there. I wanted to be with her, so I wouldn't feel so alone. The drive was only 45 minutes compared to two hours, and the shifts were shorter. I could sleep in my own bed at night rather than having to stay in a motel. This looked good, but as you read in the entry, I left him after I visited.

I'm sure you are catching on by now to the cycle that I was in—leaving him and coming back because of his psychological control over me. So you may realize that I

would be working again in Maine as soon as he could sweet talk me into it.

September 24, 2000

Well Whoa, the last time I wrote I was fucked up huh?! Well B and I did get back together after that. The last fight we had was one night when we were together & out of the blue we went to the Spinica Italia restaurant. We weren't really dressed appropriate & to make a long story short we didn't get let in. I said something, B took it the wrong way, flipped out & I left him @ the gas station near his house, then I refused to go back & get him. So he came to my house, we cried & laughed at how stupid we act & I went home with him. I think he realized how he acts & that I really wasn't playin anymore. i was done. So done. When just last week i changed my # and everything. But then went back with him. He got it when i left his ass.

But for real, we do good together, it's just like we fought for a couple of weeks. I wasn't happy, I didn't feel like the relationship was going anywhere. I was tired & ready to walk away from him - without even giving him a fair chance to show me something good cuz i was scared. I was nervous of the whole commitment thing. I know that B is good. He is a good guy. I'm not making exuces but I'm not Ms. Perfect either.

One morning when I slept over, I haven't been there in a couple of days, so we like missed each other. We woke up & he was holding me throughout the morning - and then he whispered "J, I <3 you." I'll never 4-get he was lying on his stomach with his white tank top on, his arms stretched out in front of him & I go "what" & it took him a minute to say it again, but he did. But just before he said it he kissed me on the forehead & was holding me... in my head I was like "this kid loves me" than Bam - he said it. I started to cry. Happy tears. I took a deep breathe & was so happy.

He came to my house that night after I left him @ the gas station & got me, cuz we both realized we really like each other & we are almost perfect. As one. He also learned a lot about me that night, he met my dad & i think that it meant a lot to him. B changed from *that night. We're doing good. I need to work. Maine is good. He wants me to work on getting my Master Stylist License so we can get on the ball and open a salon. I go to school on weds for the massage therepist certificate. So we are making moves. A crib* together, then a salon, then who knows!*

The other bitch thing, well - whatever, he tried it but it lasted one day. She fucked up and B said c-ya. I gotta trust him. As far as I am concered he's my man & any other bitch is nothing. We will live together & the chic can stay wherever she's at. B knows this, so it's cool. It's a business thing. Fuck the Pimp*n* shit. B ain't gonna be anywhere near the shit he's on with me with any other chic - 4-Real. His heart is right here & ya know what, it ain't going anywhere else. Ok.. Bye

*Crib = house

November 4, 2014

Anti-trafficking

I have been a part of the anti-trafficking movement since 2012. Using my voice to share my story as a survivor, advocate and public speaker has been very rewarding. After speaking, I usually open it up for questions. Many people have asked: "How many times did you leave him while you were being trafficked?" My answer is, too many to count. I can see from the above and previous entries that I was leaving him and going back numerous times, and it had only been three months since I met him. What an eye opener that is! I still remember the morning he professed his love for me. I found what I was looking for—love. Also, I was searching for acceptance, but that never came.

I ended up in this cycle of striving to get love and acceptance from him. The more money I made, the more he loved me. Now I know that the love wasn't real; but at that time, I really wanted it to be. I wanted the relationship to work because I didn't want to sell my body for nothing! I would tell myself it's for us, for B and me to get ahead and to make something out of life. And yes, he met my family. Yes, he would end up coming to their house on holidays. He was setting the stage to make it appear as if he was my boyfriend, and I believed him, too.

The massage therapy school that I attended was in New Hampshire. I was there with other girls who were going to be working in Maine as well. I paid around $500, went for a few weeks, learned basic massage techniques and got a massage therapy license. B and I took a sealed envelope to a meeting at the lawyer's office that was connected to the massage parlor, and I was cleared to work. I don't remember all the details, but the lawyer knew he was doing business with pimps from Massachusetts. That lawyer would then pay the local police chief, and that is how the brothel remained in business for so long.

As you can see, the game of pimping is based on lies, deceit and greed. I was lured in. I would end up working in Maine for two or three years. Massage parlors are everywhere. Have you identified one in your community? If so, make an anonymous tip to the National Human Trafficking Resource Center at 1-888-373-7888 or visit www.PolarisProject.org.

October 10, 2000

Well once again, I've come to a conclusion. No more. Jazz isn't happy at all. Not one bit. I hate the situation. B and I got into another bad fight sunday night. I feel like all he does is control me & everything I say is wrong. I feel like my opion doesn't count. Or if I disagree then he takes it the wrong way. Sat No friday night Maria asked me to go out to Logans Lounge & since I didn't go to school on weds I couldn't work till the next friday anyway - so I got my hair done & then B was out, Maria called so I wanted to go out with her.

B said No. - Cuz I went out tuesday. I hate that, I hate when he controls everything. I hate being restricted. So - Sunday was an all day arguement cuz B was just in a bad mood, I said something, whatever and we fought cuz I walked out of his house cuz I just couldn't take it anymore. The agravation, his voice, getting heated.

So he pulled me up the stairs, I screamed for his mom and brother to come out in the hall to make him stop, but when I grabbed on to his mothers leg for help she shook me off.

Then Mark asked me to just go into the room and talk with him. But I knew it wasn't gonna end there cuz he was still upset. I told him that I feel he disregardes what I say - & he got mad, picked me up from the shirt and threw me across the room. I hurt my back so bad against the metal frame of the bed. All i could do was cry.

I had to go to my moms for her B'day dinner and he wouldn't let me go. Then when he did, he followed me to my car & wouldn't get out for like an hour & half. We fought more, the cops came & said that someone called & said that there was a car running for over an hour, so they came to check & in my heart i believe that it was Mark who called cuz he saw how bad B was hurting me. I tried to get out of my car twice, went nutty on him. He straggeled me, then I flipped out, screamed & tried to stab him with my keys. He cried, then took my key chain picture of maria & me and left.

It was horrible, almost like a movie. I saw him today to get money to deposit, we talked, cried, laughed but I know I have to go. I gotta. For my health, mental and physical. I got bruises on my arm & back. My back really hurts. I slept with a heating pad that night. I know he feels bad, but this is something that i gotta do. For myself. No more scrafice for him when he does shit for me except, control, manipulate, hit & make me feel so bad. - I don't need that. No more chances. Fuck That.

I called the MGH* today. Tried to make an appt for a conselour. Someone to talk to. Cuz I don't have anyone. My friends? Yeah Ok. They're no help. Sometimes I feel alone, sad. I need a job. I know god will help me pull through this and give me the strength to survive. Fuck the money.

*MGH = Massachusetts General Hospital

November 6, 2014

Recognizing the Signs

The fights, the control, the abuse, the beatings, the mental torment, the isolation—it was all too much for me to handle. He was breaking me down, breaking my will, breaking my spirit. He wanted complete control over me; he would use money, violence, tears and laughter to get it.

I'm not sure if the general public knows much about pimps and where they come from. In my experience, it starts with broken relationships in the home. B was raised by a single mother and never knew his father. That single mother was the one who watched her son pull me up THREE flights of stairs. Yes, she shook me off her leg. Why? Was she used to this kind of violence in her home? Did she get beaten by her former husband? Did she think I deserved it? Was she afraid of her own son? I do not have the answer to any of these questions, but I know that B was the hustler of the family. He was out on the block selling drugs at the age of 12 or 13. He had to help support the house—his mom, brother and sister.

Selling women was his next hustle. Unfortunately for a hustler, selling a human being is not as easy as selling crack to an addict. The crack doesn't have feelings, and it doesn't talk back. But selling one woman over and over again is more profitable than selling drugs once. B was looking at me as an object, a means to an end. He saw dollar signs. I saw a guy who I was in love with. I wanted him to love me back, but I got bruises instead.

I also had a run in with the cops that night, but they didn't look beneath the surface. I would soon be meeting with a counselor at Massachusetts General Hospital, and she wouldn't notice the signs either. With that said, it is my hope that law enforcement personnel and medical professionals would receive training to recognize the signs of trafficking. Then they can ask better questions and intervene when they encounter these types of situations—because they will encounter them. It is inevitable.

Photo credit: Department of Homeland Security.

October 16, 2000

Hi, It's me. Who else! Well B went to Atlanta with Mario, Big, & Jimmy for 4 days. He just got back yesterday. I was really straight with all of this, when i called Chloe to tell her to bring my hat to work on friday so I could go pick that & all my stuff up, when she was talking & made me realize, just how easy this shit is & how much money i do make. It wasn't like she talked me into it, but she did? I really don't know, but B and I decied to give this fuc*in thing 1. ONE. UNO. more try. I told him that i wanted a percentage. like 25%. He doesn't really like that idea, but oh well. Today he said "I feel like that you should believe in me & I'll just give you money weekly, if we do the percentage thing then we might as well be business partners instead." & I said well if that's the way it's gonna work then let's do it that way. We can't get along in a relationship so be partners. He sighed & got a depressed look on his face.

Personally, B isn't B anymore. All that shit, I thought we were so good together. I thought he was such a good kid. All that love in my heart went away. He hit me one too many times for me to still like him as much as I did. That's how I am - people will fuck with me, I'll let them, cuz i just 4-get about it, but then when it's over, it's over - No more feeling. It's that simple. He fucked with me big time. My feelings, my whole fucking life. My heart & my back - No Joke. He don't love me. I don't love him. He's rude. I almost wrote arrogant but I'm not sure on that one. He's just not the one for me.

How can I believe in him? Is this all my fault? I have no trust in anyone but myself? That's terrible. But shit, how can i trust him when all he does is fuck up? The $5G's in the net -? Hello! Where did it all go? Sleeping at other girls houses. - Wow - Fuck em. all the other chicks. Then he goes and gets another chick? Why bother telling me things, then go back on your word? Little things - I pay attention to. I know no matter what he says, that I treat him like he treats me. I know that i am a good girlfriend/friend & person. I have a big heart. Sometimes that gets in the way. But I treated B good cuz I wanted him to like me & treat me good. I thought he would love me back the way i wanted - Seriously. I don't think this is going to work. He says that we need respect for each other. How can I respect someone that hits me & belittles me? No way.

I need to do something. I just don't care anymore. About B. About work. Nothing but the health of me and myself. Which I've been neglecting for a while. Something in my heart is telling me to go with Miz. Kate's friend. He's older, but right now B isn't doing me right at all. & I know that if I went with Miz it would break B's heart but oh well. He already broke mines a long time ago. I could save money, get a nice car and have no personal shit with Miz. Just pure business. How perfect. Like no strings attached. Maybe it is just a thought. We'll see what happens. Well I gotta go to bed. Work tomorrow (oh fun) As I roll my eyes. (P.S I also went to MGH & talked to a lady. She helped me realize some stuff about myself & that I am a strong woman.)

November 11, 2014

Culture of False Hope

Sex trafficking and prostitution rings have their own cultures and systems. They don't run like the rest of the world. I literally became someone else. First, it was Tami. Later, it would be Brittany because the sex buyers thought I looked like Brittany Spears. I was immersed in a world where I had wives-in-law, new lingo, and an extended family of pimps and their girls. Chloe was part of that extended family. Her pimp was Jimmy, and she had been in the life for a few years. I would talk with her about wanting to leave, and she would talk me into staying. She was probably believing and hoping, like the rest of us, that this life was all we had, and it would get better. I would find myself thinking the same thing as the years passed. Trauma specialists have told me that while I was being victimized, I had to have some hope for the future or I wouldn't have been able to survive and make it out.

Choosing up, is another term often used in this underworld. I was thinking about choosing another pimp (Miz) because of the difficulty I was having with B. I didn't end up doing this, but many girls do. It doesn't turn out as pretty as they imagined. The reality is that the majority end up getting involved with a more violent or oppressive pimp, or they just get sold from pimp to pimp. The game, or the life, is no life at all—no matter what he tells you.

November 2, 2000

Well, B and I have talked alot, I went to MGH & talked to someone. I've been seeing her almost every week. (3 times now). She helped me realize alot. I talked to B, made a chart about respect, love & relationship ideals. We also made a chart for goals & our expenses. I'm trying to fix things & make our relationship correct. And I've even noticed him change a bit. Which is good. Than Bam. Maggie leaves a note in his room one night while we were out - saying - (Love you Forever your girl Maggie) What?!! i silently flipped out. And how's this, just before that happened I went to B's house to wait for him & I went in his pants pockets & eleven numbers feel out. A bunch from when he was in Atlanta. Ok. He's telling me, he loves me & wants to make our shit tight, but he's getting chics numbers and trying to pull them. SO I ripped them up & left a note saying "Maybe when you can keep it real & foucs focus on one thing" And I left.

Then I called him & met him in Chelsea. That's when we went home & the note was there (i think) I'm not really sure, but it fucked with me. Then he said he would take care of that. Then Tuesday, we went to the JayZ concert! I'll write about that later. But N-E-ways. I called him to let him know i was ready & he picked up the phone & was like "what Maggie" all upset & shit. And I was like - Yo, it's Jazz & i just want to let you know i'm ready & he was like - "my bad. yo". Whatever... about 15 mins later, bitch calls me looking for him- WOW- Then tonite she calls looking for him - not once, but twice! Wow, after i just left his house fighting with him about her. He really needs to decied. Me or her. I already told him to put her to work but has she - No. Whatever. I'm about to leave this mutha fucker. Cuz he's not being fair. At all. Fuck the money - fuck everything.

Well. I met Jay Z!! Beanie Segal, Memphis, Lil Kim & Dj Clue. After the concert we went on the Spirit of Boston Cruise. Suzanne & I had a good time upstairs! Then B got mad at me 4 being up there all night. Whatever. I'm really upset, confused and hurt. I think I'm gonna go to work tomorrow & saturday, get money & keep alot of it. Cuz I need to pay these bills, get another job & get my life back. Cuz I'm scraficing so much 4 B. My whole life & that dude hasn't scraficed a fucking thing. Say bye to that dumb bitch or say bye to me. And that's it. Actually I'm out anyways. Fuck the money. 4 Real. I'm straight. B isn't doin me any good. - now is he? - Na, not really.

November 13, 2014

Someone's Daughter

We live in a culture that constantly objectifies and exploits women and girls. When did it become acceptable for a guy to

have two girlfriends? I cannot believe I was with a man that had one woman selling drugs for him and had another woman (me) selling her body.

I have experienced this oppression not only because I was sex trafficked, but also because rap and hip hop music fuels it. The artists we listened to rapped about making money by hustling, selling drugs and women. Derogatory sayings like "pimps up, ho's down" were used often. And I'll never forget the movie Hustle & Flow. It glorified the game of pimping. The group Three 6 Mafia became the first hip hop group to win an Academy Award for Best Original Song and the first hip hop artists to perform their song called, "It's Hard Out Here for a Pimp." I mean, really? Who nominated and awarded these men? Oh yeah, American society.

This work in the anti-trafficking field is an uphill battle for me because I'm dealing with the hearts of men and some women. But mostly, men, who think it is OK to buy and sell human beings. They use, abuse and exploit someone's daughter. That is just not OK with me. I will fight and give my life for this cause. What will you do?

November 14, 2000

I don't wanna stay. I don't wanna go. Can we get it 2-gether? See, I'm so confused. I just don't know & I don't understand. You know I don't want to stay. You know I don't want to go.

Well, that song just came on the radio & it was almost perfect. It explained my feelings so good. Right at that moment. It's how I've been feeling. B & I are over. For good. I just can't take it anymore. I'm unhappy. Very very unhappy. I need a change. A new direction.

I have an interview with a guy from Blaine Hair School. I can be an instructor! How cool! I made a resume. I think that is soo good. And I believe i can do it. B doesn't believe in me one bit. I hate him for that. I'm not a stupid bitch, I can do shit. And i will make something great and spectacular out of what i got. & I got a lot!

ME. I have alot going for me, he just, got in my head & heart, slowed me down & confused me.

But i know I will survive. I saw a shooting star last night! I wished. I'm excited to get away & start fresh. I plan to ask him for some money though, just to get me through this w/out a job. I'm hoping & I can feel that he will. I don't think that he would leave me w/out anything. Cuz the man has a heart for me. I love em, well i really like him, but he's not what I need. Or want. I mean, why? Why? All this? I can't believe i let him hit me, control me, pimp me - everything. Well - fuck him. - It's over. Sarah (my consuler) was right - to him it was like loosing a prize. She couldn't of said it any better & neither could I. Stay Strong.

November 20, 2014

Survive

Moving on from an abusive relationship is hard enough, never mind when you're being sex trafficked. I would like to say that was the end of my relationship with B, like it was the end of that notebook. I was up against some big changes, and I know that's why I failed time and time again. Think about what it would take for me to leave when I had been depending on my body to make money, depending on men to purchase me and depending on one man to provide all of my basic needs.

"But I know I will survive," was what I wrote. Can you hear the strength in my words? This was the strongest I was feeling up until that point. I was determined to go and make something out of my life. I think it had something to do with the therapist. She was helpful and encouraged me, even though she didn't notice the red flags or realize I was being trafficked. I'm thankful for today, because I am not just surviving, but I am thriving and living a full life.

To increase awareness and help families, law enforcement, medical professionals and justice workers, End Slavery Tennessee has created a list of red flags.

Red flags from http://www.EndSlaveryTN.org/redflags, retrieved 10/6/2016:

- Chronic runaway/homeless youth
- Lying about age/false ID
- Injuries/signs of physical abuse (that they may be reluctant to explain)
- Untreated illnesses or infections. Examples: Diabetes, cancer, TB.
- STDs, HIV/Aids, pelvic pain/inflammation, rectal trauma, urinary difficulties, abdominal or genital trauma.
- Inability or fear of social interaction
- Carries hotel keys/ key cards
- Emotional distress such as depression, submissiveness, anxiety, panic attacks, confusion, phobias, disorientation, self-inflicted injuries or suicide attempts
- Inconsistencies when describing and recounting events
- Unable or unwilling to give local address or information about parent(s)/guardian
- Presence or fear of another person (often an older male or boyfriend who seems controlling)
- Sexually explicit profiles on social networking sites
- High number of reported sexual partners at a young age
- Talks about an older boyfriend or sex with an older man/boyfriend.
- Uses words associated with the commercial sex industry.
- Has a prepaid cell phone.
- May try to protect trafficker from authorities, have loyalty to trafficker, not identify as a victim.
- Has an unexplained sudden increase in money, clothing or other goods.
- Is frequently truant from school or not enrolled.
- History of abuse and/or trauma (rape, violent crime etc.).

Editor's Note:

According to Norman Doidge, MD in his book, *The Brain That Changes Itself*, falling in love causes activity in the pleasure centers of the brain, and it releases dopamine. This feel-good chemical makes people feel more sensitive to pleasurable things—sights, sounds, touch and encouraging words. It also increases a sense of hopefulness. However, the highly active pleasure centers can make it more difficult for people to make healthy judgments. That's because the pain and aversion centers of the brain are under-active, and it's harder to feel annoyed or even disgusted.

Doidge explains that when two people make love and have an orgasm, the brain releases oxytocin. This chemical increases a sense of bonding and trust. The problem is that it can cause some people to be more trusting than normal.

Together, dopamine and oxytocin cause the brain to be more changeable—so it becomes similar to plastic. This increased plastic ability, or plasticity, helps two people to shape each other's perceptions, plans and self-images—for better or for worse. In the case of an adoring partner, the change can be for the better. But in the case of a manipulating partner, the change can be the worse.

Chapter 2

Diary: Year 2001

January 5, 2001

Well it's a new year! Already! This will be my new journal because the other one ran out of paper! Well, 2001. It doesn't feel any different. Life is still the same. But everyday I get a little smarter & I begin to understand the world & myself a little better. This year's resoultion is to be more goal oriented & focused. To be myself, & make sure i know why i do things. My life has changed so drasticly since last summer when I met B. I definitly grew up a little more, & see stuff in a whole different way. Life has strange ways of working sometimes, it twists & turns & sometimes I'm not even ready. I'm pretty good w/ sticking to my resolutions. Last year, I made one, to stay more fit & healthy. I did that for the most past. And the year before that i made one to not be so uptight & chill out relax & that worked. So i know i can do whatever I put my mind to. Which is a good quality I must say :) A little self assuance.

So anyways - I feel better that I am writing, I was feeling a little stressed I think i needed this, since i can't really express my feelings to anyone w/out getting a response or whatever! But i really need to get out of my house, if I'm gona work, cuz it's really messin w/ me. Lying and puttin on a front w/ my family everyday kills me! I mean, now that i've been doin it for a little while, I'm getting used to lying, but then it just slaps me in the face cuz I can't stop thinking of work, the girls, the tricks, the whole day - just replays in my mind. It's like I almost can't seperate it. The two lives are collinding. They are mixing & I really hate it. Even when i try to sleep i think of it. i even dream about it! When I'm w/ B, I think about it. Not all the time but enough to bother me.

I try to seperate myself from him & not stay there so much cuz my feelings are so confused. Is he my lover or my pimp? Hello! It's not working cuz it's hard to deal w/ him wanting other chics, all that shit. He feels bad, but what can I do? Going back and forth, my house, his house, work, boyfriend, pimp, business partner - all that shit is putting a toll on me emontionally.

Maybe when we finally get a place & we're more stable, I'll be able to deal w/ it all a little better! I hope cuz I'm really testing out my disipline & will power right now. Just how strong can I be? How much can I take? Well I'm just gonna reach for those stars & get em!!! Goals, goals, goals. Focused. Tell em to Holla @ me man. I'm focused man. Stay focused Jazzie. And I'm doing Tae-bo tomorrow!

November 25, 2014

This Is How I Survived

According to MentalHealthAmerica.net, "Dissociation is a mental process that causes a lack of connection in a person's thoughts, memory and sense of identity."

This is what was happening to me and to many victims when they are sex trafficked. It is the brain's way of protecting the person. If I didn't dissociate, I probably wouldn't be here now telling you the horrific details of my life.

In that dark time, writing was therapeutic for me. As you can see by my journal entry, *"I feel better that I am writing, I was feeling a little stressed I think i needed this, since i can't really express my feelings to anyone."*

Miraculously, I saved those journals that contained many details. These writings can help you understand the victim's mindset, and they have been very healing for me.

The mental health issues that victims face are complex. As we exit sex trafficking, we have to learn a new way of life that is really foreign to us. We call it the square world—the world of regular people working 9 to 5 jobs. In my early recovery, I remember feeling like a fish out of water. Because I was so used to manipulating, lying, shutting off (dissociating) and being someone else for so long, I didn't know how to function in the square world. I used to tell the sex buyers that I was attending Northeastern University in Boston and prostituting to help pay my college tuition. I think they wanted to believe this so they could sleep at night and feel like they were helping me.

If you are working with girls or women who are fresh out of the life, you need to offer a lot of grace and compassion. The old way of operating—lying, manipulating, shutting off— doesn't serve them well as they try to make it in the real world. How to build healthy, safe relationships needs to be modeled for them. Treat each one of them like she is someone's daughter—because she is. And she is worth it.

January 18, 2001

"The intellect is always fooled by the heart"

Francois de La Rochefoucauld

(A quote I found inside a Bacci candy wrapper)

Well Hello There... SO my life right now Sucks. I am confused & hurting so much, inside and out. B & I are having problems. A couple weeks ago I told him that i had to stop my feelings cuz loving him like I do is impossible with the way our life is. I can't help but get jealous when he is with another girl or wonder who's on the phone and all that. So i told him i had to stop cuz it was driving me crazy.

So now we're not getting along. At all. 4 the past couple of days I've been crying, left work early, I'm driving him nuts. I don't want to sleep over as much, I hate kissing him cuz then i get all weak inside. Cuz my feelings are so strong. Last night & times before he keeps asking me, if he makes me happy & i tell him that yeah he makes me happy but "our lifestyle" doesn't make me happy. He was saying that he knows how I feel, that he knows he's really never made me happy. Like, one day it's good - really good, then the next it's over, that good day doesn't last & he's right, cuz i can only pretend for so long.

I feel bad like, Ok. Now what - Now what do I do? End it? Where the hell am I gonna work?? How will i like it, a new life, my old life.? I don't know what i wanna do & all the time I sit here & stress like, where do i wanna be? What are my goals? Should i just live 4 today.. or what? Whoa I think I gotta leave B alone. Or should i just friggen move in? HELP HELP

December 2, 2014

Messy Recovery

Looking back and reflecting on this entry reminds me of the power of my emotions. When I was with my trafficker, we were intimate and that automatically linked us together with strong soul ties. Lust had set in, but I was fooled because I thought it was love. Hence, there was the confusion that I was experiencing. This all worked in his favor because I couldn't make up my mind whether I should stay or go. I also did not want to go back into the square world because it seemed boring, and I thought I would never be able to make it in real life. This false sense of security in money, lust and love was keeping me hooked in.

Isolation and brainwashing are two tactics that traffickers use to keep women trapped in the life of prostitution. Even though the victims are the ones making all the money, they become dependent on their traffickers. Leaving and getting a regular job is messy and difficult for women, especially if they got involved at a young age, have a drug addiction, mental illness or have little education. What about the women

who have children to care for? There aren't enough beds or safe homes for trafficking survivors and even fewer places are designated for trafficked women and their children. So let's HELP THEM!

Listen, getting out of the life is hard. I stand here today as proof that it is possible, but it takes a strong, healthy community. Women who have been through sex trafficking, or forced prostitution, need our care and support. They need our talents and gifts. They need our money. They need our time, energy and love.

Lastly, when women and girls receive healing and recovery, they need to become empowered survivors. If you are a part of an anti-trafficking organization, I ask that you strengthen survivors by inviting them to be keynote speakers. Reimburse them for their time, effort and wisdom. If you don't, they will feel exploited all over again.

Actual diary page.

January 31, 2001

Well it's me - who else! I worked today - it was slow, & I'm tired. I wanted to sleep @ B's but he said that he was goin into town - so i would have to wait. So i said 4-get it. Went tanning and came home. & it kinda hurt my feelings that i couldn't stay there. But it's maybe better if i stay home so i can go to tae-bo in the morning. If I get up!

Sometimes I think i am too sensitive?! Am I? Do I take things to the <3 to much? My feelings easily get hurt when someone i care about does something. I have a lot of pride & it gets hurt a lot & easily. I think I'm so tuff, but I'm really a mush inside.

Well anyways, B and I are "on" again. Jeees, I can't get my mind right! But i figured hey what the hell - get the apartment and just try it. I can always move back home, Even though i doubt I ever will. But hey, ya never know. School is almost over. 2 more weeks of this shit! A lot of places have been getting busted lately - so we gotta be careful. Oh well.

I think that B and I will have fun living together. It will definitly be a big change & so new to both of us. But I think that we will have a good time. I just hope everything works out. Cuz so much has happend to me & we've gone through alot, it hasn't been easy. not one bit. But the ride seems to be getting smoother as we go. (knock on wood) He's a good person & means well. But it's just hard for me to deal w/ everything when I'm still not used to the game & especially cuz I'm not stable.

But I think it will all change when we move. We got a couch (again) & we are on the hunt for an apartment. So I'll probably write again after I've moved! Hopefully. Pray - Well C-ya

P.S. B and I have been together for 10 months! Almost a year.

December 4, 2014

Anchored Hope

The definition of hope is to want something to happen or be true and think that it could happen or be true.

I was hoping for a lot. I was hoping that B would love me, cherish me and not make me sell my body. I had to have hope; otherwise, I would have never survived. There were times when I felt hopeless, and I wanted to die. I remember being in the car with B, driving on the highway and wanting to open the car door and just roll out. I actually envisioned it, but I didn't have the courage to do it. Instead, I stayed. I numbed my mind, body and emotions. My heart was sick, and I was dying inside. I was hoping for something to take ALL THE PAIN AWAY.

The Bible teaches in Proverbs 13:12 that, "Hope deferred makes the heart sick, but a dream fulfilled is a tree of life."

During my recovery, I have learned to put my hope in Jesus. This has given me an anchor to hold onto during rough times and peace for my anxious heart when I need it. I am watching my dreams unfold, and I am amazed at how far I have come.

My favorite place to walk.

February 12, 2001

Hello it's me! I'm just sitting here waiting for B to call cuz I need to meet up with him, I need money to deposit 2 morrow. That's what I hate. I hate when i have no money on me, & i gotta meet w/ him, Bla, Bla.. My checks have been bouncing, cuz I sometimes let him deposit the money for me, & then he doesn't do it on time. It's really starting to get on my nerves! (sigh) Me & B.

Well B and I finally spoke with Maggie. I finally got to explain things 2 her. & I let her know exactly where i stand & the rules of the game. She seems OK, But I still don't know. Now instead of a 2 bedroom apt. We are getting a 4 Bedroom house! Whatever. I feel uncomfortable living w/ her and her kid. But no one else seems to think that it is a problem. So Whatever. Yo, I think that's fucked up & now that I'm writing this & thinking, I'm really getting mad. I hate this shit! Cuz I have a feeling that things will never change. I'm gonna put all my money & time into this house, then hate it.

B just called & I'm gonna meet him @ his house in a half hour. Ya know, I feel like crying. I'm really fed up. Today he went & put all the money down & filled out papers. & he's been so rude for the past couple days, he must be stressed out. Cuz I really can't stand him right now. Whatever. Then he wants to put her big ugly Tv in the living room & i'm pissed cuz I think that it's gonna make the living room look ugly. & then Maine won't let her work cuz there's already to many girls, so she's not working! wow. WHATEVERRRRRRRRRR. I gotta go cuz my life is shitty right now & I FEEL LIKE SCREAMING.. I HOPE I FEEL BETTER.

December 9, 2014

Lingo

To help you understand the rules of the game, I will outline the lingo or language that is used. In the back of the book, there is a glossary of terms used in the life. I said before that sex trafficking happens everywhere, and it's in plain sight.

But often it is hidden and incidious. Therefore, it also has its own culture, language and laws.

February 20, 2001

Well hi, It's tuesday-1am. I'm about to go to bed. Last night, Maria and I had an awesome night.. We went to a club in Rhode Island. B was pissed but, oh well. We had a good time. Today i just chilled. Me & Ma were home all day. I learned how to crochet in Maine, So I was making a blanket. I <3 it. I also went for a fitting for Katie's wedding. I'm happy to be in her wedding. I'm glad she found a good guy to marry.

So anyways. Life is Life. Nothing new but The new thing is B wanting to move to East Boston & I am having a heart attack cuz I think that is to close to my family & shit. So whatever. We're in the process. We'll see what happens.

i just wish life was easier than it has been 4 me for the past 9-10 months. B & I will be together a year in early March! I can't believe it. It's gone by so fast. It's flying right back to by me. I hope I can catch it soon! Shit! Well anyways I'm tired. I gotta go.

December 11, 2014

Secret

My emotions were always all over the place. I was excited about this new way of life because it was fast. But I was feeling beaten down by it at the same time. My life was anything but ordinary. There I was in a friend's wedding—a very special and normal part of someone's life. She was a good friend from school, and we were still in contact, even if it wasn't constant. She had no idea what was happening in my life. I kept it a secret from friends and family because of shame and fear. I so desperately wanted to be normal and act like everything was fine in my life. But as we know, it was far from safe and healthy. The isolation was getting worse. I

stopped working at the hair salon, stopped attending college and rarely saw my friends. He was gaining more and more control of my life. Confusion had set in. It was about to get real dark.

March 3, 2001

Hello there. I'm just sitting in my room, on the floor listening to my new CD's that I got. Jay-Z, Slikk the Shocker, Public Announcement, Sparkle and D.J Clue. Well anyways, life is still life. B & I are doing good. We are not moving to East Boston & Maggie is not gonna live with us. Well that's how it is now.

B and Maggie got into a fight & I thought maybe just maybe she would leave, but a day or two later, they were handeling buisness again. So that wish didn't come through. Then she brought back stuff that he had @ her house! I'm sorry that makes me feel uncomfortable. If I'm his bottom, then hold on, she shouldn't be doin all his stuff, like paying his cell phone bills, doctor appts, insurance, all that shit. Granted he did whatever with her before, so now she's just still there, but if he was such a pimp then why wasn't she working before? & why isn't she handlen her buisness right?! She's tellin bitches that B's her boyfriend/man that they've been 2-gether for mad years. B just checks her on it, but i wish i could just leave him alone totally, or she would leave, cuz with her around, I feel tension, competition, pressure, uncomfortable.

I can't be that down chic, #1, Bottom bitch that he wants me to be. Cuz I got her doin things and gettin in my way. & yo i swear 2 god, it's not just cuz she's a woman that's doin buisness with B, it has nothing to do w/ jealously. It's that I don't like the history they have, & the way she feels about him. I can't stand that she has a picture of them in her car - calls him all the time, comes in his house, knows his whole fam, all that. I'm not the first, I'm the second trying to be the first. Yeah the first to hold him down in this game, but not the first bitch there.

Well today I was supposed to go to drivin school, but of course I was late & they wouldn't let me in, So B had to do stuff, I felt bad cuz i hate when I do everything around him, then Blam. When he's gone, I'm lost. So i went & got a haircut and put some cornrows in the front of my hair, went tanning and bought some CD's.

Well B promised that we could chill 2-nite. Go to the movies or something. He couldn't see me earlier cuz he was busy. See that's what I mean. Now what?! It hurts me, cuz it's not like I think he's lying it's just I'm not 100% sure what he's really doing & it drives me crazy! I feel like he lies to me, cuz he thinks telling me the truth will hurt me. But really, him not telling me hurts me even more. Cuz before you know it he'll call me & he'll be @ a strip club or something - either that or he'll come home @ 1, 2, 3 am or never get home. But if that was me!? Forget about it! I'm tired.

I'm gonna go get my stuff @ his house cuz I left it there thinking i would see him later. But nope! He's probably with some bitch! - whatever. I feel like crying & getting mad and leaving him. Cuz when he doesn't give me what i need, I get very aggatated & feel shitty. So whatever. I have no money to get gas to even get to his house. I want to go to the museum tommorow w/ Brian but B is probally gonna die if I really go! He doesn't understand that Brian is just a good kid & we're friends. He doesn't understand. He's to over protected. Protective of me. We got into it the other day. I told him i didn't want 2 be with him, returned everything i bought for the house, he came to my house & I jumped out of his car @ the fire station, ran, he got me, the cops came, we cried, made up & now here i am today. Still not all happy. Better but not really. I know he's a good person but the game is hard 2 deal w/ cuz of the way i feel about him.

But when i get that terrible feeling inside. I try to remember how & why I'm hear, & what i want to do. When I feel myself going to the left, I try to stop & think, get back to the center & get focused again! I try anyway. Well whatever. I hate maggie. I hate when B isn't with me, I also hate when i have no money. & no love in my life. - I love when I'm happy and comfortable. Some day J. It's coming! :)

December 16, 2014

Worth

After the last entry, I laid the foundation and wrote about the game. The way of life for a pimp is going to strip clubs or the mall, nightclubs, etc. One of his main goals in life is to find vulnerable women and girls who he can pull into his stable. B had me as the bottom bitch, and he was trying to build his career as a pimp.

I was trapped in a situation that had taken over my life, and I couldn't find the way out. As you can see, he used my greatest need to control me. Love and acceptance were my greatest needs then, and they still are today. I'm grateful that I can find what I need in God and by serving others in safe and healthy ways. I have realized that I cannot find it in people, places or things.

I experienced manipulation and brainwashing to the max. My trafficker was isolating and controlling me in many ways, so I would become dependent on him. I was beginning to think I would be nothing without him, and he wanted it that way. When we would fight, I would leave him. He would come to my house, cry and tell me that he would change. One of his best lines was, "No one else will love you like I do." Another line was that I was special to him because I was his bottom bitch, and the other women didn't mean anything to him.

It has taken me years to believe I am worth something and that I can be loved for who I am. My worth does not come from "doing" or "being anything" for anyone. I am simply worthy because I am fearfully and wonderfully made by God.

March 14, 2001

Well hey. I'm in work & I need to write. I haven't wrote in a while & i need to vent. Maria is on vacation. Suzanne is whatever and B is B. Sometimes i just can't understand my life & what is going on. B and I are one mine minute so good & then the next I'm saying in *my mind how much i hate him. I just don't get it. Really.*

Like just today when we were on the phone, he was like "yeah I got some chic trying to holla @ me". And I'm like Oh yeah - that's good. But im in my heart or somewhere i feel like crying. Then i was like well i'm am I sleeping over & he was like I'm not sure cuz this chic might be breaking herself. She works with Maggie. Then that made me feel even worse. Like, oh now Maggie is pullin bitches. - & bla bla.

Well were where the hell can i find bitches - The ones @ work have better Ho lifes then me - Well some of them. They know the game a hell of a lot better. We don't even have a crib for me to bring em [other girls] to. I'm so disgusted. & He better find somewhere to live soon. Real Soon. I really think that this is my problem.

I'm so anxious. I feel like he isn't even doing anything fast enough. Well i mean I know he wants a crib - but what the hell.. I know our shit isn't perfect. Isn't easy. I hope when we get a crib, life will be so much easier. Well I hope. It just seems like it's so hard right now. It's been hard. So how much worse can it get? It can only get better right? He tells me he "wants me here 4-ever... That he loves me. " I do all this. All this for you, Jazz." And Everything i sacrifice, my body and my life - 4 him. & me ? Do I wanna spend it with him? What do i want? Where do i want to be? Where am I going?

Yeah I like this life. Cuz now I'm used to it. To even think about going back 2 being square kills me. I mean i can't even see myself going back. B and I have been 2-gether 4 a year now. I've been working 4 almost 9 months. I just don't know? I gotta chill. My feelings gotta seperate. Big time. I feel so depressed & unhappy. And all he wants is 4 me to be happy.

I keep saying that I'll wait to move to see if I'm really all set with him. But it's taking so long & something and hurting me so bad inside. I don't even talk to Maggie anymore. That friend shit lasted a week! Cuz I heard again that she was telling people B was her boyfriend. bla bla. I tried to leave B, I changed my number and returned everything i bought 4 the house. So she doesn't have my new #. But before I changed it, when B & I were fighting she called me & asked what happened & I told her that it was none of her buisness & that was that. So since I heard she was still running her mouth - I have no respect. I'm straight.

I just hate everything & I'm just dealing with it. That's all. Just keep waiting. Hoping that something good will happen & something will go my way. Cuz I've been real good to this dude. I've done a lot. I got a good head on my shoulders. & I need to be supported the right way. When he can't give me what i need - I'm straight. I need to seperate my feelings & handle business w/ him. Whatever. (Sigh) Please Help!

December 19, 2014

Attention

When sex traffickers have multiple women in their stable, there is bound to be jealousy, backstabbing, fighting and chaos. It comes with the territory. Most of the time, each girl is fighting for the pimp's attention. She wants to be the best in his eyes, the biggest money maker, the prettiest, etc. That's why he also may have the women call him Daddy. They look to him as the one who will care, comfort and protect them. In reality, we know this does not happen. Sure, he might take one of his girls out shopping or take her to get her nails done, but this is just part of the manipulation. When he gives this kind of attention to her in small doses, it keeps her hungry for more. This makes her work harder to please him and causes her to dislike the others who are trying to do the same thing! It all blends together and creates an environment where the pimp has all the control and the women suffer under his authority. He abuses his power.

April 18, 2001

Another Day! Still the same shit. Easter was good. B came over my house and ate with my family. It was a beautiful day. The weather was great.

Well, work is work. I'm still having a hard time w/ my feelings for B. I moved into his house, probably 3 weeks ago. I was tired of not knowing where he was, when he comes home and all that. So we decied that I should move in. I'm uncomfortable staying there cuz it's not my own space, I mean I share a bathroom with 5 other people, which kinda skeeves me. Plus I bring laundry home for my mother to do & I don't even stay here.. That's rude. Then there's no food in B's house - like, no breakfast food, lunch - nothing. I feel funny when he's not there and I am. I'm frustrated. B is too. We need a crib.

Then last night i told him all that and how I felt & I told him that I wasn't in love w/ him anymore. And I feel bad that I told him that. Well it's true. I mean all the shit i deal with. I gotta face the facts. I can't be in love with a pimp. He's not my boyfriend. But that's how I've been treating the situation cuz that's just how we are together. & It's sad cuz we could really have a beautiful, intimate relationship. We could really love each other. But it's hard to love someone the way I love B.

When he does the things he does. Maggie, calls him w/ issues all the time. Fighting w/ him about stuff that has nothing to do with buisness. See, this game got us all fucked up. It's a damn shame. I actually thought of marrying B. Making a commitment. Figuers this happens to me. And I said this from the begining. That's why I've tried to leave B a million times allready. I give a fuck about the game & the money.

I care & love B with all my heart. That's what fulfills life. LOVE. Money buys things but it can't make you happy. Well temporary, but not 4-Eva. B is a great guy. I just wish he'd give up this game soon.

December 24, 2014

God's Love

Even during one of the darkest times in my life, I knew love would fulfill and satisfy me. I just didn't know the source of that love. It would come from God and more specifically through Jesus. It says in the Bible that God himself is love. 1

John 4:7 says, "My loved ones, let us devote ourselves to loving one another. Love comes straight from God, and everyone who loves is born of God and truly knows God."

I remember when I was in early recovery, I was seeking the answer to my deepest questions about God, myself, who I was and how I was going to make sense out of all that happened to me. When I found God's love, I finally felt alive again. Have you found that love and acceptance?

May 24, 2001

Hello, it's me. I'm home! I moved back my stuff from B's. I just couldn't take staying there anymore. I was so uncomfortable there. Everything from hating when B didn't come home to be with me, to not being able to cook anything for myself, to hating when i wake up in the morning & seeing his ass still sleeping. It makes me sick. Really. I hate being w/ him, cuz I feel like he's not the one, I mean I hate having a man that does nothing. I mean, I work. I clean. What! He doesn't even have a job! I pay him! I just can't let that be. When i know that there are plenty of bitches out there doing shit on there own.

I'm tired of him flipping out, putting his hands on me, yelling about money, making me do everything. Him trying to control everything. Like what the fuck. I've been working 4 almost a year. I have hardly anything. I lost my earring and he kicked my ass for it. My bracelett is still on layaway! He said that i can get my own crib, bla, bla. But i still don't want to deal w/ him & all his shit. I hate maggie so much. Just cuz of the way he handels his buisness w/ her. He argues w/ her. I've been there when they're on the phone arguing. She doesn't work @ a spot. She does calls! Yeah, so while I'm in a whore house all day, she's out doing calls & then this other bitch he knows that knows maggie, only wants to escort, cuz he says she's not really spot matirial! PLEASE!*

There are 2 spots i can name off the gate that she can go to! Whatever. I'm just so straight. I want to finish school & then open a salon, work in a salon in the mean time. Now i just have a little more game, then I did last year. But, i learned a lot. I learned a real lot. So that's all I got to do is survive. The last year wasn't a waste. It was a learning experinece! So what doesn't kill me can only make me stronger.

It's hard to let go of B. Cuz he's a good friend. & if it wasn't for this game - then i believe that we could have a great realtionship! And it's to bad, but I'm not gonna give up my life & let someone else control it. Just cuz the realtionship we got. I just haven't felt myself in a long time. I can finally get back to normal! I can't wait!

One more thing, I started weight watchers & I'm doing great! I've lost about 5 pounds allready. & I only got to loose 10-13lbs! So I feel good! And I also got a tattoo. I feel a little crazy for doing it. But B said he really wanted me to show him how much I love him. I felt like it was right for that time & now that I don't want to be w/ him.. he'll always be in my heart... So we will see what happens.

*Spot = illegal brothel that is concealed as a massage parlor.

December 30, 2014

Redemption

Not feeling like myself was something that I would get used to because I was surviving and not living life. Once I got into recovery I would tell my therapist that I felt unplugged. I had no other words to describe the way I was feeling, but I knew I was not being myself. I felt lost.

Without drugs in my system, I started working on the 12 Steps in the rooms of Alcoholics Anonymous. This not only gave me a revelation on how to live, but also I got connected to my Higher Power. I finally felt plugged into the Source! I love how God meets us where we are. I found Jesus in the backseat of a car with a few older women who told me about Him after a Sunday morning church service. This is not only awesome, but also redeeming! I've done a lot of unholy things in a backseat. So how appropriate for God to meet me in the backseat when I was filled with the stain of sin and shame from my past and riddled with feelings of guilt and depression.

At that time, hopelessness had set in. I had my former pimp's name tattooed on me. His permanent hand-print was on my body. I had been branded, labeled and stamped.

But God—He had a different plan for me. Thirteen years later, I was blessed to receive free removal of the tattoos from a local skincare business. They help women and girls who have been tattooed while in the life of sex trafficking. They remove the permanent marks of the past, so women start fresh!

I am in the process of being renewed from the inside out. All those feelings of shame and guilt have been washed away by the power of the Holy Spirit living inside of me and transforming my heart to be more like Jesus. I am reminded of the Bible verse in Ezekiel 36:26 that says, "I will give you a new heart and put a new spirit in you; I will remove from you your heart of stone and give you a heart of flesh."

June 7, 2001

Hey. Well I have a headache! B just left my house. He came here cuz I was supposed to go to work 2-day & he was supposed to call @ 8:30 & he didn't. Then when he calls at 9:30, he was in Everett & I like flipped out, cuz i feel like he stayed with her last night. Or something crazy. I feel so insecure w/ him. I can't trust him @ all. So he came here & we just talked for about 4 hours. I cried, he cried, all that same shit. Then he's so pissed that I went to Miami. I went to just get away from him & all I did was talk to him the whole time!! So Hello??!

I've come to the conclusion that love has taken over. & life is so ironic, that two people, find each other, fall in love, but they are in a situation that includes NO LOVE. I swear, I could make a friggin movie! Called "The Love of the Game" I <3 B & He <3 's the game. MONEY. I understand his desire, his determination, but now that we're in <3 why does he still gotta pimp me? I mean, I know thats how we met, but I know that the game just isn't for me. I feel so shitty and I feel shitty a lot of the times.

I wish B & I could just be together. Figures, I feel in love with a pimp. Hello. & this isn't the first time I've said this. I remember the first day I told B that I <3 'ed him. We were @ a food place & I just yelled it out & he was like WHOA! It was so hard not to <3 em. He's a great guy. & I told him today - that he's gonna make some girl really happy. No doubt. It's just - how do you hold on to something that isn't right? I don't want to hold him back from anything. I want him to live his life & I feel like I'm no good for him. I feel terrible.

I just wish, I could deal w/ everything but I can't. I hate that I gotta share B & "break myself" everytime i work, then ask everytime I want something. It just sucks. I hate it! It's hard. I want to be his woman, and that's why i tattooed "B's First Lady". I'm his lady. i want to be that one.. that holds it down. But I don't want to be his ho. I don't want to work for him. It's just so hard. & it's a terrible thing. & It's a damn shame 2 people can't grow together because of this stupid lifestyle we call "pimps & ho's" or "the game."

January 6, 2015

Blooming

This entry shows how much self-awareness I had even while being manipulated, abused and sex trafficked; how much love I wanted to give even though I was being exploited; how broken I was; and how much emotional pain I was experiencing. All that, and I was still wishing.

I believe this entry alone will help non-survivors understand the complexity of sex trafficking. Most important, it will answer the nagging question that many people ask. "Why doesn't she just leave?"

It's a deeper issue for some women because the trafficker could be the only person who ever treated her special or made her feel loved. Think about a girl who is sexually abused as a child. If she is not helped at the time of the abuse, her internal dial and self-worth is turned so low that getting paid for what was taken from her as a child seems like an upgrade. That is why women coming out of the sex

industry need to be seen as someone's daughter. They need healthy, supportive, safe and empowering relationships, so they can bloom into the women they were designed to be.

My wish is to see them reclaim what was stolen.

June 9, 2001

Well another day. I just read everything I've written in the back, trying to understand my life. I'm trying to understand what's going on?? OK. I got in this game @ the begining 4 money & to live good. I liked B's whole attitude & he was real to me. I was used to messing with guys with no money, no dreams, nada - B had it all & I liked it and he liked me. So, Ok I got down, I even got Maria down. I told her look, these dudes aren't trying to take from us, they are trying to build w/ us. I straight told her some real shit and she decied that it wasn't a good idea 4 her sooner then I could realize what it was doing to my life. But the first time I tried to leave B was when I had enough and he hit me. No one has ever laid a hand on me like that in my life.

I remember telling Joey that i needed a man, someone to love me for me & not a pimp. What can someone you pay do for you on an emotional level? I mean, really. It's foolish to think. That's why the #1 Rule of this game is "NO LOVE." B and I discussed this a long time ago. He said, "J, don't catch feelings for me." Yeah Ok dude. don't catch feelings for me! It's only natural when two people like each other for then to act on it.

And I remember telling B, you're to good to be a P. You're no good at it. You're real and you have feelings. Pimps don't do none of that stuff. P's throw game at you. You threw real shit @ me, that's why we are in love. So now B wants to take advantage of that love we have & I've tried but then it gets me so confused. I want to literaly go insane, hurt someone so bad,, so that they can feel the anger i have inside of me.

B thinks cuz i love him then our shit should be that much tighter! But it makes us that much seperate. Every time he talks to another bitch, or about another one, I get so angry inside & i want to say to myself, What am I here for? I hate this kid. Really, I say this all the time. But then I quickly 4get about it and everythings ok 4 the moment.

Today I was supposed to go to work again - I drove all the way there, then left! Last night, B asked me to stay w/ him, i said no, even though i kinda wanted to. He got a little upset but then said, "fine you don't have to." - I can't understand why we talk about him falling back & us not being together so much, then that. Like hello, that confuses me big time. I know we <3 each other. So how do you stop hanging out with that person or stop staying over their house? I think we are cheating ourselves by not loving each other. & He says we are cheating ourselves by not making money together. So how do we decied what to do?

--- Had to stop writing... B just called, he is in the net w/ that chick & he wanted to know what was going on with us.. and we always go back and forth. I'll say something, then he'll have an answer for it. Right now @ this very moment, I'm so confused. I'm so confused being just Jazz and B for so long then this trying to get used to more. I know that he is trying. Trying to make this thing work. But it's me. Do i really want it? do i want to work? I think that i am just being extra hard on myself. I want B to be with just me. That will never happen. Should I just stay with him?

But i noticed when i just stay with him i get bitchy towards him, cuz i just can't be his ho. his bottom. i gotta be more. I really feel like I am loosing. Cuz i'm not happy. Even though he insists that i should be happy to have a dude that cares about me the way he does, espeacilly in this game. Which i mean, yeah it sounds good. Being his ho & having your p love you like that but something just ain't right. That's why the #1 rule is what it is. Love fucks up the game. I mean i always need to answer & question everything. Like B, if you <3 me, then how can you pimp me? I know that i wouldn't sell nothing that i loved. So that's why questions like that get in the way.

He doesn't really get it. I feel so much anger, jealousy, insecurity. I feel like i am not good enough. B needs more than i can give him, that's why he has other bitches. Then of course i don't want no bitch doing better than me. - competition. How the hell can i function?

What do i like about getting my own crib? First I need to stop thinking about how hard it would be to get a crib w/out B- Cuz it is possible. Always remember you don't gotta be a ho, to live. If i get my own crib and hate it, B will definitely go crazy and not let me go. or will he? I'm afraid of being able to make up my mind. I can be indecisive. Especailly when i am confused about the big picture in the first place. Cuz that's what I am confused about. The whole thing! Do I leave or do I stay? Oh my goodness. I just got a thought to call Joel and tell him I'd come in for the night shift.. And thought - girl you just left there in tears and came home.. why would you go back?! So how do i decied & what is wrong?

Hello OUT there! Can anyone tell me what's going on in my head of confusion? I love em, I hate em. I love em. I hate em. I am driving myself crazy. B won't give up the game and I don't want to be a prostitute. So why are we together? He won't give up the game cuz when he met me, the plan was for us to get paid and be together but not in love. But B says that love don't pay the bills. - money does. Maybe this is a test to see how far i will really go? I can't change B. But why did he get to change me? I totally changed everything. The hole thought process, my mind, my actions, everything. I just didn't 4get how to love someone. He wants it all. My love and money. And look a year later. Still hardly nothing. no progress.

I thought I could change him or that other chics wouldn't phase me - yeah ok. it;s almost like having a boyfriend that cheats on you! I'm writng alot and i still haven't made a clear desicion. I can't even friggen spell. A couple of months ago I wanted to regain my freedom. I started doing things to better myself, then I moved in with him, got fed up w/ all that and came home and my mind is still telling me something just ain't right.

But my heart is saying - just <3 the kid & work. My heart and mind are constantly fighting. I don't even know what my gut feeling is. I wish I could then I would go with that. I'm a sad sole. Really. I hope B learned a lesson. They say "Never fall in love wit em and never try to make a ho your house wife" painful lesson, indeed. I learned just bc you are feeling someone, you don't let them change your mind about everything you stand for.

I remember hating the game. I thought it was for lazy bitches with no direction. Then B, got me into the net - it's weird how things work out and how quick life can change. There are a lot of people who can help you and alot that can hurt you. It's hard to tell the difference when what's hurting you is also loving you. It's almost like an addiction. B makes me feel good but the aftermath makes me want to die. The consequences for loving a pimp are not easy to deal with. He's fucking other bitches and giving them his time! And to hear him on the phone giggeling with another bitch drives me crazy! Then i get angry inside and pick other things to complain about or tell him something like " I don't love you anymore" Trying to hurt his feelings.

I feel better that I wrote this all down instead of say it to B. Because he just won't understand. At least the paper can't say "Are you really doin this J" "Are you really leaving me".. I think i know my decision, i just gotta go with it. I am a little scared of getting a job. I feel so burnt and hurt by B. Who ever said it was wrong to put a little love into the notorious game of pimping?! Oh, B did. Well I guess some rules never change. it's just the way it gotta be played. & it's all good. I ain't mad. Just sorry i feel in love with the wrong guy.

January 8, 2015

Grace

That was a long entry, but it is very clear about the confusion and inner turmoil I was dealing with. If I could go back and speak to that sad soul, I would tell her that she is indeed confused and angry because she is being manipulated and abused. The man she is in love with doesn't love her for the gem that she is. I would pour mercy and grace into her life by being supportive and loving her right where she is. What would you do?

June 9, 15 & 17, 2001

Well it's 9:41pm. I wrote earlier & I really vented. I just left B. Literally. I told him that we had to let go. We huged, hugged & he said. "it just won't be the same w/out you J." And i felt like, i know it won't be the same. Then he calls me & says "just give me a 2 week grace period"! Hello! I just left you - so for some reason i said OK... & Now. It's June 15th & i went back to work on tuesday, weds, & today for a half day. Yesterday i met the other girl, milly. Maggie met her - through the service - she's been working in the net. I'm having a little break down, and now B is spending the night w/ her there cuz it's her first night staying there & that thought is totally fucking w/ me. I feel like having a heart attack. I'm getting real angry.

It's June 17th 01. 10:41pm. i can't seem to get my feelings right or ever finish writting. Today I realized that i really can't handle this anymore. I can't deal @ all. Something is really buggin me. When I think of B w/ Milly. I get so fuckin - anxiety, angry. all that. So then today i talked to Suzanne & told her that I wanted to choose Magic & she said "girl don't do that - No way" & I said I'm just real scared, that I won't be able to make it out there. & She said "You have a good strong head on your shoulders and you can make it." She kinda gave me that extra boost I needed. Cuz I feel so scared. - I can't even figure out the word. I just don't feel confident w/out B. Can I make it? Of course it will be hard @ first. Getting back to normal. But I can do it. I mean, I'm the one making the money anyways! SO i just need to get ready for this change.

I think B wants to let me go. Cuz he see's how bad it really is. He just doesn't want to say it. Cuz of course he really don't wanna.. We need to talk, he called & said that, so i got a gut feeling that, that's what it's gonna be. Cuz it really ain't working out. Everything is colliding & making us fight constantly. I've been through so much, that I know I can say Bye to him & it doesn't even hurt as much anymore. I'm getting over him mentally. Now, I just need to get over the feeling of being nervous to be on my own. I am overwhelmed. I will find something to do. I will be fine. I know i will.

SO we'll see. -But what I want to know is -why did he hurt me? ugh, I'm tired.

January 13, 2015

Protection

I don't care if a woman has been sex trafficked for a day or for five years. The feelings of low self-worth and fear are imminent. Having been sold, isolated, beaten, manipulated and raped made me lose every ounce of dignity and confidence I had, which wasn't much to begin with. That is why I stayed month after month, year after year. I did not believe I could make it on my own, either in the square world or in the game. I just didn't know where to turn for rest. The lure of his love and financial security kept me trapped.

Today, I can thank my God for His safety, protection and deliverance from that life.

I love the Bible verse in Psalm 23:7 "You are my hiding place. You will protect me from trouble and surround me with songs of deliverance."

June 30, 2001

Well today is saturday & it's 1:35pm. I'm waiting for B to come pick me up. Suzanne was supposed to pick me up 4 work, but she didn't - well anyways. Drama. So my car broke & hopefully it will be ready on monday. It's gonna cost almost 2 G's. Well anyways B and I.. Oh well what can i say. i guess i just have to get used to this hole thing & i have to accept it.

That's my problem, i'm having a hard time accepting everything. And I'm driving B crazy. But what am I going to do? I just lost my train of thought cuz Suzanne just called & told me that she left work already.

July 10, 01 - Well another day. It's tuesday & I'm at work, I found this paper & thought i might write. I've been a little stressed lately. B plays to many games with my emotions & I'm straight up tired of it. I can't take all the little white lies he tells me & swears that he tells me those lies cuz he gets nervous. - I'm like - nervous - and he's like Ya - cuz I like you & I'm afraid to tell you the truth cuz everything i do is wrong! & I'm like whatever - Cuz I like you but I don't lie to you - I'm so straight with him. & if he's not handling his buisness right, then there is no way i can handle my shit. Right? For real. It ain't right & yo I can't wait to see what happens when he moves in! I'm just chilln & doin my thang! It's all good.

July 21, 01 - Well what a day. What a stressful day. Since last night & the last few days, months.. B is doin his thing. Ok. Now i can understand Maggie and the other chic are in Conn. He drives them & stays with them for right now cuz it's all new. Fine - I get fustrated when he's sooo busy & he has no time for me. He stayed with them two nights in a row. I feel so lonely. Like, why can't we hang out? When? like? He was like, "J, I know why your fusterated & i understand, but your my bottom & your not supposed to be complaining." But I'm like. "Yeah Ok B. Handle your buiseness that's fine but don't forget about me. I'm the bottom so what i gotta wait 4 everything."- wait to be with you - wait to get time w/ you - Yeah OK. It's upsetting me I feel so left out. Alone.

Like it started when he left me one morning when i only was there for like 6 hours, cuz i came after work & he had to drive both of them & i was like, it's my day off & you gotta leave me to go drive - two of them - I was hurt. & now all i want, is to spend some time. Like go to the movies & spend some real time together. But i can't cuz he's always busy. So cool. Well today we got into it a little, and he got all pissed & started getting really mad. Now I'm even more upset.

I didn't even want to come to work today & i called him & told him i wasn't. Then I called back and told him i was. Then he calls me back later & says " i can't wait to see you tonight" & I said "oh yeah @ 3 in the morning" And he's like - "to make up for lost time & you know you're my baby".. bla bla.. I'm like stop sayin that shit, cuz what you say and how you act are two different things & you confuse me. Then i pissed him off when he was like - Oh, I'll be there when you get off work, cuz they are getting a ride home by someone. & I was like yeah but then you gotta take them home & leave me at 3am & he was like "what the fuck- why are you acting like that I'm going to be home when you get there!"

-- But I just want one hole night w/ him, but i guess that's too much to ask. I hung up on him. He calls me back and tells me I need to get my shit together... And I'm like "I do, I know what I'm doing!" - Just to much shit and whatever. It's all good. B- just do your thing. Like I said before, I ain't mad - just give me what i need to survive in this game. It's not easy. Cuz I don't ask for much just some time. That's it.

January 15, 2015

Transformed

Sex traffickers use mind games, manipulation and lies to keep the victim under their control. I've mentioned before that sex trafficking is like domestic violence on steroids. I say this because of the intense shame the victim feels from being exploited. The constant chaos, confusion and abuse take a toll on your mind, body and soul. That is why so many domestically trafficked women become addicted to drugs. They might start using to numb the emotional pain or the trafficker might give them drugs as a way of keeping them under control. Either way, it is a reality.

As I write this today, I'm excited to share that I will be starting a Survivor Support Group at a women's halfway house! I feel there is a great need for the women in drug recovery to hear from a healthy survivor. This will help them begin to deal with some of the trauma they have experienced. My hope is that lives will be transformed, and they will break free from the burdens they carry.

July 27, 2001

Well Hello. It's 12:15 am. Today was an Ok day. I notice i only write when i feel bad & ya know that isn't good. i mean it sounds like i live the most terrible life. But i know that life is only what you make it. & I've decied to make my life full of happieness... Happyness. I CAN'T Spell! Well at least as good as I can make it. I've realized so much.

I'm not angry. I can understand the game and B a lot better. I know where i stand & i know that what i'm doing now is for the future. I'm B's bottom. No doubt. I got it tatted on my body. Ok. So that's good. I <3 him & care about him, he feels strongly about me. So now the other bitches? So what, I don't care. Maggie, a little still but we'll see. I'm just waiting to move & once that happens, I know that everything will just fall into place. B is moving in the right direction.

i actually feel good. anxious but generally good. God has granted me this strength. Finally... Cuz i allowed it to happen. i was ready to accept what i cannot change. I've done awesome w/ weight watchers. I've lost 15 pounds! 138 to 122. I feel great. I was even thinking about getting implants.. I swear i will never gain that weight back! i feel and look awesome. So now i'm so aware of my eating habits, it's great. I feel healthy. Even though sometimes, I'm very thin, i feel fat. I hope I don't get all crazy & shit. Well i just want to stay this way. So i will take care of my self and stay healthy.

My birthday is coming!!21 !! I can't wait. Hold on, i got a phone call. It was B. he's on his way to the net - & one bit of me says whatever w/ an attitude. And the other bit says - so what, he's doing what he's gotta do. Oh well. I just know that we are getting along. I'm getting stronger everyday. I have faith.

January 20, 2015

Building Muscle

I hated being sex trafficked. I had no tangible way of getting out. I was beginning to accept the reality of my life. The way I

began to cope was by losing weight and developing an eating disorder. I would force myself to throw up after meals, not only because I always had a knot in my throat and stomach, but also because I made a vow to myself to never gain the weight back.

While working in the massage parlor, I had to keep up with my appearance because I was competing with at least 15-20 other women every time I worked. A lot of the women I worked with had breast implants and were very attractive. The pressure was on when a sex buyer came into the lounge area to choose a woman based on her looks and his interests! I also had a quota to make. Therefore, I needed to get picked during my shifts! My trafficker put this pressure on me to look good, but he became jealous when I was working out too much at a local gym. Working out and the obsession with my body was how I got through a lot of days. I would end up fitting into size 1 pants! Being able to control what was happening to my body made me feel safe because the rest of my world was pure insanity and abuse.

No matter what, I was getting stronger. Every day. Little by little. But when I wrote this diary entry, I was still far from the time when I would be strong enough to escape.

August 16, 2001

Well. It's me. i was just organizing all my writtings & stuff. I found a new thing. I want to start reading. I found some books I'm really interested in buying. so i hope i get time to read them. Since i like to read sayings and quotes, I'm gonna buy a notebook to write down all the ones I like. Like make a collection of quotes! So anyways. Tonight my mom is having a cake for me! My bday is monday! I can't wait. 21. Finally.

Well everything else is fine, I'm just trying to survive in this world. Hopefully we are moving Spet [Sept.] 1. & I've lost 15 lbs! I'm so happy. And I'm definitely thinking of implants. B keeps mentioning it. I would have to go down to Florida bc it's cheaper and the surgeon is really good.

So hopefully after we move things will fall into place. I need to move so bad. I can't wait to actually. I will finally feel situated & comfortable. I will feel @peace. I know I will.

January 22, 2015

Reading

I was 20 years old and found a new thing called—reading! I must have done very little of that all through my school years. :) In reality, I was trying to surround myself with positive thoughts. I would end up making that notebook. I still have it, and it is filled with empowering and encouraging quotes because my grandmother would give me her old Oprah magazines. I would also get into a lot of self-help books by Iyanla Vanzant. Those books and quotes combined with the prayers of my two grandmothers are how I slowly began to see myself worthy of more than "just trying surviving in this world".

Did you catch the fact that while I was being sex trafficked, I was still living at home with my family? My mother had a birthday cake for me. My family would come to celebrate my 21st birthday. No one knew what was really going on in my life. If you were sitting with me now, the next question you might ask could be, "Where was your pimp?" I'd smile and say, "He was sitting right next to me, smiling and enjoying the cake."

Lastly, moving out of my parents' home seemed to be the best option because I could not continue to travel to Maine and lie to them about where I was working. The guilt and shame was intense. I didn't realize that moving out would give my trafficker more control over me.

September 15, 2001

Ok. Well today was ok. Nothing different. All i know is that B is really controlling. He likes to control everything i do. He tells me I ask to many questions & so then i stop. I tell him, look i don't give a fuck about what you do, where you go - Nothing. Ok B. Cuz when i do care, I'm to much in your buisness, so - Oh well. I totally have shut him out of my heart. - Really. Cuz you can't possibly <3 someone, when they don't love you the same. Especially a P. Na, either, i give ya all i got, or i don't give ya shit. None of this in the middle shit.

You want me to be your bottom bitch. OK. I do that & then it's I don't care about you - Ok so now i call you, ask you what's going on - make my plans around yours, but I don't care, you get up late, it's my fault. You don't get your shit done - Na dude - you need to get your own shit together, & do shit yourself. It's not my fault that you don't have a license. - What, What else do you want? - Yo, like I said before, we don't live together, so this isn't easy. He always has something to say - all i want is to be friends w/ this dude, that's it. - I don't care to fight, nothing.

Whatever - is my answer to everything cuz I'm so tired - so tired of arguing over nothing. Whatever. How am i supossed to deal w/ everythin in this life style & love you - Na it don't work. i lost love. I really think so. I didn't love him, i just wanted to be wit him. i like him no doubt. But i've learned the hard way. love don't work in this game. Oh well. & he knows it. I've shut down. Sorry, but I can't bear. & he has this big thing about me not respecting him, well how do you respect someone when they don't know what respect means? Does he even respect himself? He doesn't respect me all that good - & he never understands when i tell him the truth. He says - whatever.

He tells me he'll call - he doesn't call, he says 1 hour, it's two, he says jump and I'm supposed to say - how high -. Na, see he got a issue cuz he likes me. He thinks he lets me "get my way" w/ things. And he says " I come out my mouth" alot and that " I am out of pocket". & That's how i disrespect him - So ya know something, all he's wanting is for me to sit back - shut up & do what he says, essentaily. & ya know something, that ain't me. Not one bit. So we'll see B. We'll see. It's a shame. A controlling Dude. - I hate that. I let you live your life, then let me live mines. Peace. J

January 27, 2015

The definition of freedom is: the power or right to act, speak or think as one wants, without hindrance or restraint; the state of not being imprisoned or enslaved.

B was controlling me with money, promises to change and his love (or what I thought was love). This is the classic way a pimp/sex trafficker gains control and keeps control over a victim. At this point, anger and resentment was the fuel that pushed me toward my freedom. But actual freedom wouldn't happen for a few more years. Still, I see this as a small step toward my exit.

If I had been using drugs at this point, like many women do, I wouldn't have been able to gain anything besides a growing addiction. Drug addiction is the sad reality of what happens to many women and girls who are caught up in the life. Because of this, sex trafficking in America is very complex. It takes many different service providers—such as treatment facilities, recovery centers, mental health providers, trauma specialists and the community—to join the fight for her freedom.

Editor's Note:

In a study published in the September 2005 issue of *Neuron*, people who were about to earn money showed increased activity in the nucleus accumbens—the brain area associated with reward, pleasure and addiction. Compared with brain scans of cocaine addicts and of people experiencing orgasm, the brain scans of people about to earn money were nearly identical. Further, the research by Camilia Kuhnen and Brian Knutson showed that the pleasure circuits in the brain can override the reasoning circuits of the brain—the frontal cortex.

In another study that was published in the December 2015 online issue of *Brain*, researchers found that when the brain's reward center was stimulated, people were more likely to show risky behavior.

Simply handling money can reduce social and physical discomfort, and that condition can last for up to ten minutes, reports researches Xinyue Zhou, Kathleen Vohs and Roy Baumeister in the June 2009 issue of Journal Psychological Science.

In the October 2016 issue of *Nature Neuroscience*, researchers Dr. Tali Sharot and her team found that telling self-serving lies desensitizes our brains and gradually escalates and may encourage us to tell bigger lies in the future.

Lying for personal gain causes the brain area called the amygdala to produce a negative feeling. However, this emotional response fades over time as a person continues to lie. By watching the decrease in activity in the amygdala, researchers could predict bigger lies. In other words, as a person stopped feeling bad about lying, the bigger their lies became.

Chapter 3

Diary: Year 2002

February 4, 2002

Well I'm back home! I did it. I went through with breast augmentation! It wasn't as bad as I thought & after the consultation with the Dr. I felt more confident & comfortable. After the procedure was done - it was the worst feeling coming out of the anesthesia.. I hate that feeling so much. But being home now, with a tight bra on and the stitches look good. While B & I were down there we chilled, he was good, except when he totally disappered all night after the surgery. He is such an asshole. But really. What did i expect? I mean he was doin all right then he leaves with his cousin & doesn't come back til 1:30 in the morning. It's kinda funny cuz it just helps me to know exactly what type of person he is - self centered. Very about self.

So anyways Suzanne came by yesterday with balloons and cards. She's so nice to me!! So I'll be out of work for two weeks or so until the stiches come out on the 16th. Gotta go work on the blanket I am crocheting for my cousin. Bye.

January 29, 2015

Travelling

After moving out of my parents' home, I moved in with my trafficker. Living a double life was mentally exhausting. At home, I was the daughter they thought they knew. At the massage parlor in Maine, I was Tami. Moving out, I was enslaved. And I was isolated even more.

My brother Chris was ten years older than I, and he moved out and traveled the globe for many years. He was making sure he stayed far, far away from our family. At the time of this diary entry, he had settled in San Francisco. His story is his own. But to help you understand the dysfunction surrounding me, I will say that coming from a large Italian-American family, being gay and having HIV wasn't something he talked about at holiday family gatherings. It was his secret, and he confided in me. The pain he was trying to escape was evident in his lifestyle. He was searching for love and acceptance through sex for money, drugs and relationships. When I visited with him, I saw that we were living almost identical lives. Both of us were searching for love and keeping things a secret, hoping to just survive.

Sadly, my brother paid a heavy price for that. He died from a drug overdose on June 22, 2006 in Manhattan, NY. He will always be remembered for his exuberant personality, intelligence and stunning looks. As I mentioned, he traveled the globe and touched many lives, but he will remain in my heart forever. May you be resting easy, my brother.

Chris, my brother.

March 17, 2002

Well, Whoa, I haven't wrote in a long time. So anyways. Things are semi-the same, but different. B and I moved to Malden in Dec. Christmas was good. New years also. My Ma & Dad had a little bit of a hard time w/ me moving out, but it's ok now. My life consists of work & keepin the house clean! Fun huh? Well I went to visit Chris in Jan, it was a good time. A little stressful with him being sick & meeting his boyfriend! But he is doin well. Suzanne and I are going to Miami in May on Memorial Day weekend! We can't wait.

Well livin w/ B is.... Whatever. how's that. I basically can't wait to be on my own & not under the control of a man. I honestly hate my life @ times. But i gotta do what i gotta do until it's my time to leave, I'll be here suffering to some extent. I made the decision to be here so.. B - pimp - Me - Not mixing. It really never did. So I take every day as it comes & pray for a brighter future. -- alone, or w/ B? Who knows. I doubt he will ever change. He's just not the type of man, I would want to spend my life w/. At one point I thought I did, But not after all the pain & mistrust he put me through - Na, I'm all set. I'm better off alone.. No trust = No Relationship, So i'll write again. Peace. J

February 3, 2015

Body Image

Two years ago, I took a trip to Florida to see the same plastic surgeon. The doctor told me that women don't normally come back to get the implants taken out. Once they have them, they keep them for life. That wasn't the case for me. I knew that I had to have them removed. That's not who I am anymore. I also didn't want to take those double D's into my future. And, let's be honest, I was so tired of men talking to my boobs rather than to my face.

Since last year, I have found a new sense of freedom in my body—just the way it is. For the first time in my life, I am satisfied with how I physically look. I am healthy, very active and a size 12. Also, I can wear button-down shirts. :)

I just love how God has redeemed so much of my life. I was once truly lost; but now, I AM FOUND.

May 28, 2002

Well i haven't wrote in a long time, it seems like i don't write anymore. I used to write a hole lot. When i write it clears my mind. I don't really tell anyone how i truly feel, I just write it. So when i do it makes me feel better.

So does that mean that I've been doing better or that I'm ignoring my problems? Well what a mess I'm in right now. Suzanne & I went to Florida for the weekend & it was somethin i never want to remember again in my life. My intentions were going to just chill on the beach & have a good time, kinda like clear my mind. I wanted a massage, I wanted to swim with the Dolphins, scuba dive... Did i do any of that? - No - We layed on the beach one day, shopped another & went mental the next. Like a big ass i fucked it up by not calling B when i came home from being out @ night, I just went to sleep - Big Mistake cuz he flipped & told me to come home. So now that fucked everythin all up & I felt like Dying. I didn't want B to be mad @ me & he was on vacation.

February 5, 2015

Safe People

Gone are the days of not having anyone in my life to confide in. This is one of the biggest reasons why a person may stay trapped in the life of trafficking and prostitution. Not having a safe person to turn to for help keeps them isolated and hidden. Now I know that when a woman is ready to exit the commercial sex trade, all she needs is one safe, supportive person to confide in for help.

I am so grateful for the small, supportive and safe group of friends in my life. Finding that group has taken time and effort. It didn't just happen. I believe it is a necessary part of recovery. These people have loved and accepted me—right where I was. They didn't need anything from me. They were not using me for their own purposes. Most important, they showed lots of grace and forgiveness.

Last year, I was in some difficult relationships, and I read a great book called *Safe People* by Dr. Henry Cloud and John Townsend. I recommend reading it if you have come out of abusive or unhealthy relationships. It not only tells you how to find safe people, but also how to become a safe person yourself. I am still a work in progress. I have not arrived at complete maturity, but I am a lot further then when I started.

How about you?

Can you be a safe person for victims and survivors who look to you for support? Or, if you are a survivor, have you created a support network of safe people?

June 13, 2002

Why Why.. I feel so Bad right now. I'm sitting here on my floor crying as usual. i have that terrible feeling inside my body. I want to scream or something. I need to Escape this. I hate it. B is really hurting me. It hurts so bad.

Today on my day off he messed with me all day. He gave me a hard time about everyting then tells me were gonna go food shoppin - & then he calls @ 9:30pm - like ok you can go -- cuz he's gonna be with two chics he met in N Carolina. So then i come home from shoppin, I want to shower & go to sleep but I can't cuz his company's showering. What is that? I tried to have a good day. He lets me go do a call by myself but then i gotta wait for him to go food shopping? Hello? I don't get it. But whatever.

I don't get my life. Or B @ all. Why did i stay? Why did i say ok? This is gonna be the longest 2 years ever. We made an agreement, 2 years & a joint account. - I keep having dreams that my Ma knows what I do. I feel uncomfortable. I need strength. I really do. i gotta suck it up and get through this. I need to detach myself from him. My feelings are way to involved.

I hate the way he treats me. He thinks he's so nice. He doesn't understand how he disapoints me all the time & how bad it hurts. I need, I wish to have a better life some day. I gotta stop all this pain. All this hurt inside isn't fair. I must like tourturing myself cuz I stay. Go- stay. Go - Stay? Why? Can someone please tell me, why I do it? Why is this happening? I hate to see him w/ other girls so bad I want to kill em. I get so angry inside. Please make it stop. Girl, get strong. - Like you know you can. please.

I stopped crying. Breath. C'mon Jazz. get it togther.

I wish someone could understand me. My words and feelings.

February 10, 2015

Empathy

Those feelings were very real and intense. Three years later, I started using drugs to numb the pain, only to find myself in situations that led to more abuse and a growing drug addiction. This is very common among sex-trafficked women. My colleague at the U.S. Department of Homeland Security said that in 2015, all the domestic women who they served were addicted, except two. Did you get that? All, but two. This is why I am starting a women's support group at a halfway house that serves up to 18 women. Not all of the women in the program will have trafficking or prostitution as part of their story, but they all have pain.

I was crying out in this journal entry for someone to understand my words and feelings. Today, I can be that person who has compassion for women coming out of the life, and I can understand their words and feelings. Sharing my story in a transparent manner gives them hope because they see the woman I have become. I believe survivor

mentorship and peer advocacy play a big role in helping victims become overcomers.

At times, the woman I have become amazes me. Just yesterday, I spoke at the 53rd Session of the Commission for Social Development at the United Nations in New York! The title of the discussion was *People First: Community Responses to Human Trafficking.* That was something I never expected to happen. I think unexpected blessings are the most exciting!

It has been a long, hard and messy recovery for me, but I wouldn't trade it for my best day in the life.

July 7, 2002

Ok I'm heated. What the fuck. Once again. B has disappointed me. The motha fucker hasn't slept home in 3 nights! Not 1 - 3. Ok July 4th I left him at the party cuz it was late & i had to wake up in the am. But also he was ignoring me all day & those two phony bitches from D.C were there so I was all set. Then he tells me he'll be home - Never shows up. Ok, The next day, Friday, I go to work, he says are you aggravated with me & I say yes. So then he says, can I take you out on sunday to make it up to you? Yeah Ok. i said. Then fri night i come home. He says I'll see you later - Never comes. Sat he calls me while I'm @ work, Hey I got somethin for you when you come home. - I come home & does he? NO - He comes homes take the trap & the keys to the truck, gives me some kisses while I'm sleep & then leaves.

HELLO. HELLO. HELLO!!!!!! He thinks he can say sweet things to make up for the fucked up shit he does! Then I came home on Friday night & saw all hair weave in my bathroom & I knew that those chics were here so I asked him- so the chics were @ the house? & he says no, Dougie, Big and Big's chic were. So I said - the white chic was with Big? & he said yes. LIAR. LIAR. I said again so the chics weren't here? No, Jazz, why? - Cuz they made a mess & i wanted to know who it was. Bye Jazz Bye. Click.

He hung up on me. What the fuck was that? Get caught in a lie or what. I fuckin hate him. I really do. He is such a liar & tells ya whatever he wants you to hear. Regardless if it's the truth or not. He is full if shit. My family was having a BBQ yesterday & i wanted to leave work @ 4 to go. But since he was acting like a dick I missed my chance to leave. So I had to stay in the whore house all day but he does whatever he wants. Whenever he pleases. Yeah Ok. Fuck that. Why do I have to suffer? I don't get it. I give up.

February 17, 2015

What If

Do you know why selling young girls and women is more profitable than selling drugs? Think about the drug dealers. They need to purchase the product, sell it and purchase more drugs (or re-up). Now, think about a trafficker, they don't have to re-up. They just continue to make a profit off the same product, which is a human being! When they have more than one victim, their profit increases and their investment decreases.

What is feeding this vicious cycle? It's the demand for sex, the result of broken families and failed systems.

Men were the buyers in my situation, and they are still noted as the majority interested in purchasing sex.

What if healthy, safe men invested their time in teaching young boys to be gentlemen and respect girls? What if men were to rise up and become the defenders and protectors of young girls and women? Imagine if our world had just a few more dads who spent time with their daughters and reassured them of how much they are loved.

What if healthy, safe women became mentors to young girls and modeled what healthy relationships looked like? What if moms modeled confidence and respect for their bodies? Would that show their daughters that self-worth comes from who they are, not just what their bodies look like?

It will take the whole community to be involved at various levels if we want to see modern-day slavery come to an end.

What are you doing?

October 19, 2002

Well hello. Today I'm in a mood I wish i could always be in. I simply do not care. B is B. Period. I have no horrible emotions today. I basically stayed the same. B didn't come home last night. he was over Maggie's & told me he'd be here but never showed up. Anyways when I woke up at 6am & he wasn't here here my mind started wandering. I finally feel asleep last night & then had a dream that B and I were in Mexico & we were in trouble.We got into a car that was under survaliance for a drug bust. - We got dropped off @ a terrible house & i got shot. I was bleeding bad & the police were looking for us. B was upset, then we finally got help. I think i died & he came back home. Then I woke up. I read in the dream book that when you dream of danger, that means you could unhappy w/ others @ home or have bad buisness. & if your in love than it will grow (not good). I 4-get the word... But damn weird ain't it?. Dreams really do mean a lot. I didn't stress all day.

So anyways 2 more chics got down over the past months. There ok. I mean Erica seems like her & B - Well she definitely likes B more than she's supposed to. & even the other chic, Vanessa noticed - so I know it just isn't me. So we'll see how this goes. Maggie still bothers me & B keeps telling me I gotta be more

friendly. Whatever. I understand why I gotta smile @ her - but honestly I don't like her @ all. period.

I'm just waiting patiently for my day - my time, my chance to go and live my best life. w/ or w/out B. it doesn't honestly matter anymore. I'm going to school, working 4 days, dealing w/ B & his bull shit and these bitches.. One is living w/ me - and ya know - whatever. B & I haven't been intimate in I don't know how long - weeks? a month? & when we do, I feel like he's like that with everyone - it's not the same. I see him differently. totally. Oh well I guess you grow - either together or apart. - I know we'll do just fine. getting a business, hopefully a salon is coming soon.

In september it was 2 years @ the health club. Time is going by. I'm 22 yrs old. It's a young age - but I live an old life. No doubt about that. B takes a lot of energy out of me. I try to stay as positive as I possibly can. I love life, I love myself & I want to succeed. I know I will.

February 19, 2015

Esteem

I was patiently waiting for the chance to leave. I didn't realize it, but when I started attending college, it built my self-esteem. I was working hard, and it was paying off. I made the dean's list and thought to myself, I'm not as stupid as he says I am. Sadly, when I graduated I didn't feel a sense of accomplishment because I was too numb to feel anything. My major was business management because my trafficker thought it would be a good idea for me to know how to run a business. He kept promising that we would open a hair salon or some other business. Basically, it would be a front for all the money he was making from pimping.

The most astonishing thing about sex trafficking is that it happens all around us, but it's invisible to people who are not looking for it. I was being trafficked and attending a local community college. I was 22 years old, paying with cash for each semester, driving a Mercedes Benz and wearing

expensive clothes and jewelry. It went unnoticed, but I wasn't identifying myself as a trafficking victim either.

The massage parlor where I worked was in Kittery, Maine. It had been in the community for over 20 years. In plain sight, but ignored.

All of that is to say: Please try to be aware of your surroundings and who you come into contact with. You never know what could be going on in their lives. If you sense that something isn't right, then it's probably not.

December 23, 2002

Hey. Well it's two days to Christmas. I can't wait as usual. So N-E-ways I haven't wrote in a while. I don't seem to be writting as often anymore! Is that good or bad? - Maybe I just don't have enough time. School was absolutly awesome! If I could spell! But i truly loved accounting. It was such a challenge for me. I got an A for the course grade. I can't wait to get my report card!

So I got a kitty! B totally hates him & I feel bad. I love the kitty so much. He's the best. He's all black so I named him Benz! Perfect! B almost made me give him back, but hopefully he can just deal with him a little longer until the spring when he can go out. I'm writting messy & my hand hurts.

So that girl that got down a while back.. She's an asshole. She caused DRAMA on Halloween & then the other night B took Victoria and I to King A's for a drink & she was there w/ some other chic. When the chic left, she came over to our table and was looking like her normal unhappy self. Then we tried to talk to her - but she ended up acting stupid as usual. And told B we were making fun of her the place she works (King A's) & that she felt disrespected... Bla Bla. So we got into it, B whacked her right in front of us, that is the second time she disrespected me & that's the second time B whacked her. The bitch is so jealous of me, it isn't even funny. She has some issues & B was straight with it. So he told us to return, or keep the stuff we got her for Christmas. Cool w/ me!! She was stupid. I almost can understand that she's a square, just learnin the game, but damn Victoria has been around .. what 2 months? She's straight, chic did a 360 w/out no problem. Maybe a lil - but nothing major at all. So bitches @ work even noticed her, looking all miserable. I hate bitches w/out any self esteem or confidence. I told her to get a backbone, I couldn't help it. She pissed me off.

So the kitty is lying right here w me. I love him. I got B a chain w/ a diamond cross for X-mas. He loves it. He bought me the piece I had made & whatever else i don't know yet. - oh - and a digital camera that i love.

B is not home yet. What else is new?- He is unbelievable. He drives me nuts. SO if & when i get a laptop maybe i can write in there instead of writting on paper. probably better that way,. Well now I'm sleepy. Gotta Go.

February 24, 2015

The Cat

The innocence of waiting for Christmas was still a part of my young life, but abuse was the reality. I don't even remember what that girl looked like—the one my trafficker whacked in front of me at King Arthur's. That's probably because watching other girls get beaten was something common.

King Arthur's was the local strip club. It was considered the hot spot, where pimps could find women to groom and then exploit. I don't remember the second time he whacked her in front of me. I guess I was just happy it wasn't me that time. I was feeling a little better about myself. Some self-esteem was developing because I was doing well in school. But let's face it—I wasn't anywhere near confident. I just wasn't the new girl.

I had moved from a place of almost daily emotional and physical torture to being B's bottom bitch. I was going to school, working at the massage parlor, cooking, cleaning, running the household, teaching my new wives-in-law how to prostitute, etc. The focus wasn't so much on me anymore. Obviously, he stayed out often and let me be alone in the house. I got the cat because we had mice in our house. I fell in love with the cat because I was always alone, and he made me happy. I won't tell you about the abuse my cat endured.

Benz, my cat.

Editor's Note:

According to a 2015 study published in the journal *PLOS ONE* by Dr. Valerie Voon, the scanned brains of men who identified themselves as having a sexual addiction showed activity while watching pornography that was similar to that which was found in people with drug addictions. The patients described themselves as having substantial difficulty controlling their sexual behavior and significant problems in relationships and their lives.

In response to the pornography that was viewed, the younger men in the study showed greater activity in the ventral striatum—the brain area associated with processing reward and motivation. Until a person reaches their mid-twenties, controlling compulsivity and risk taking requires more effort. That's because the frontal area of the brain—the thinking and decision-making area—is still developing.

In the July 2014 issue of *JAMA Psychiatry*, Simone Kuhn and Jurgen Gallinat found that when study participants viewed sexually stimulating images, activity in the brain's reward system was significantly lower for frequent and regular pornography uses compared with those who seldom used pornography. Also, their findings showed a decrease in grey matter of the brain (brain cells). The researchers interpreted the decrease to be the result of long-term pornography consumption. Kuhn surmised that "subjects with high pornography consumption require ever stronger stimuli to reach the same reward level."

Chapter 4

Diary: Year 2003

January 9, 2003!

Well it's Jan 2003! Whoa, time flys huh? Well Christmas was good. I got a neckalace made. I <3 it! A Louis Vuitton luggage bag, a digital camera, a coyote fur beautiful jacket or coat - whatever you call it. I feel like it's a little big for me, but it's the style. - I can't wait to get my grades from school!! It's taking so long. I'm all registered for the spring. I go back on Jan 21st. Writting II, management, marketing & accounting II is what I'm taking. & over the summer my goal is to learn spanish & I mean learn it! My new years resolutions are: to stop speeding, learn spanish & do yoga once a week.

I Love my cat. He is sitting right here w/ me! B isn't home yet - what else is new? Well that chic is gone & Victoria had problems w/ her son's father so she went back to D.C for a while. She's alright. Not bad. We went to foxwoods 4 New Years. I wasn't to excited this year to do anything like the past years. I guess cuz I know that it will be the same ol' shit & I've definitely stopped drinking so much. Suzanne was their with her man, we chatted a little. She must think we're cool. But she knows how I am & that means no, we aren't friends but we can talk here & there @ work n whatever.

So another aspect of my life - my brother is still driving me crazy. I sent him an Armani Exchange hat and scarf for X-mas but I sent it to the wrong address - Duh. He still wants to buy me a ticket to go out there for my gift.

I just read last years resoultion & it was to be more goal orientated & to know why I do things & don't ya know - I did exactly that w/out even knowing! I mean yeah, I was goal orientated. I wanted to stack & get the hell outta here! & I did and I know why I was doin it, cuz I hated B & the way he treated me & I hate the game. Then I fell off & came back.

B and I stacked over 17Gs. Just like that. We were talking about getting a salon or something. It was all good - but now all of it's gone. It's B. He's bad. But what do I know?! I know we will succeed.

March 3, 2015

Grateful

Stacking (making lots of) money, moving out and coming back is what I did. It was a vicious cycle. I would pack my bags and go home to my parents' house. I moved back and forth so many times, they stopped helping me carry my bags.

The problem with returning to my parents' house was that B knew where to find me. I would change my phone number, only to give it to him when he came to see me. I would unpack and stay a few days until my trafficker would show up. He badgered and manipulated me into coming back to him. He would cry and tell me how much he loved me and that he would change. Anything I wanted to hear, that's what he told me. I wanted to believe him because I wanted him to love me, and I thought I loved him.

When I wouldn't go back with him, he became aggressive and violent. Putting his hands on me and saying words like, "You will never be anything but a ho. No one will ever love you like I do because you're a dirty prostitute." He made me doubt myself by saying, "How will you ever live a square life again and make minimum wage?"

I believed his lies because I *felt* what he was saying. I felt dirty and ashamed. I didn't know I had worth and value. I was working on it by attending school, but the addiction to love and money had me in its grips.

I am so grateful that I know my worth today. It is based solely on Jesus and what He did for me, what He did for all of us. By His wounds, we are healed!

Isaiah 53:5 states, "He was pierced for our transgressions; He was crushed for our iniquities; the punishment that brought us peace was on Him, and by His wounds we are healed."

March 6, 2003

Well i defenitly don't write at all, or enough! It's 1:35 in the morning. I'm about to go to sleep, but I thought I'd write a little something. SO life is life. & today was a aggravating day @ work anyway. Suzanne really gets on my nerves & i can't believe i was friends w/ her! Oh my God really she is sooo stupid. Like i don't even have a word 4 her. I feel so much more positive & confident w/ out her around. I feel so good that i don't have to listen to all her "drama" Everything in her life is drama & she is a pain in the ass. She gets so jealous when I talk with to Lisa. It's not even funny. I like Lisa, i mean she acts funny sometimes but look @ her man! So - she's cool though & Suzanne hates that we talk! She is very insecure, i hate that.

So i started boxing lessions w/ a guy @ the gym. i go on thursdays after school. For 10 weeks~ I <3 it. It kicks my ass & it's a real challenge. It's great and Lisa joined too! Tina and Debbie are really good too. I like to talk to Tina alot. She's a cool lady. She helps me out w/ working out & shit. & Debbie is just a really good person. I like to talk to her, but sometimes I feel like she tells me to much! Which is Ok, i'd never say anything but Jesh! So *work is work & i can't wait till this is over. i can't wait till B & i are comfortable and able to chill & relax.*

School is good. I'm going to the MGH for an evaluation 4 my A.D.D, i feel like i need help cuz i really have trouble w/ reading & staying interested w/ what I'm reading. So it should be good. I'm having a hard time w/ Accounting 2, so I'm trying to get extra help from my Act 1 teacher, cuz he was awesome! My teacher, now sucks.

So this is probally the first time i didn't write about how bad B is or how I hate him! I just realized that! Oh Shit!! Well i lost one of my earrings. I'm so upset. It's the second pair! I'm pissed. Hopefully I'll get another one. :) or another pair :)

My brother is doing good. He's working out and trying to stay healthy which is good. He keeps buggin me to come out there, but i just don't know. He aggravates me. But I <3 em. & the next trip I take i really want to go to Vegas. Well, Nevada to work. Cuz B and I want to try it out. Make some dough!

The health club sucks lately & I'm trying my hardest, but w/ school, i can't get there till 4 & B is a little aggravated w/ that. & i feel bad. So we'll see what happens.

Ok I'm getting really sleepy. My benzie is snoring I <3 em. My kitty.

Also, Victoria is gone! She never called - nothing. She disappered! What a dumb bitch! SO i tossed the rest of the shit she left. oops - sry Vic but oh well. She left shit that she probally doesn't like anyway. But i just don't get it? I mean why did she do all that? Why didn't she just say she didn't like it? Weirdo!

March 5, 2015

Hoping To Be Noticed

I was seen at Massachusetts General Hospital numerous times, not just for my ADD but for many gynecology appointments. Recently, I looked back at my medical history. It's obvious that something was going on in my life because I visited my primary care physician almost monthly. Since I've been out of trafficking, I have seen my doctor only once a year for regular physicals. No one in the medical field noticed what I was going through. My doctor seemed more concerned about filling out forms and keeping the appointment running efficiently. Looking back, I wonder if he had stopped and took a minute to have a genuine conversation with me, would things have been different. Today I share my story with healthcare providers for this very reason. It is vital for them to be trained to identify the signs of trafficking because they are often the first or only contact that victims have with the outside world. Again, I urge all of us to look beneath the surface. Trafficking victims are in plain sight, but hidden.

May 25, 2003

Well, it's a sunday afternoon & i just got done cleaning. The laundry is in the wash & dyer. B came home @ 9:30 this morning after he told me he'd be here last night. Nothin has changed. - This is my life. - I was in Vegas this week, went to the Chicken Ranch in Pahrump, Nevada. I made plans to go there 4 10 days & i came home in 3! There wasn't any business out there either. Slow - just like here. I definitly would of stayed if there was $. If I lived there - I'd work there just like how i work @ the health club. I wish i could of stayed & came up* - like we want to. B & I are so fusturated. We want to open a business so bad - It's so close. It's just getting 2 the next level. That's so hard - the black benz got into an accident, so now we're looking for a new car. Which is good. But a pain in the ass. B told me that I could pick out the next car & we both liked the CLK Benz. Now he's changed is mind & he wants the S Class. Which is a nice car but I feel like he constitly tells me one thing then does another. So whatever he get is fine w/ me. - I mean we'll get a Benz regardless. So oh well.

But anyways Victoria sent a letter in the mail saying how she was sorry 4 not calling and just disappering -- We couldn't believe it. Kinda weird. SO I kept the letter. I don't know why but I did. I guess i liked Vic. - She was alright.

So now i've decied that since Ralph @ work is giving me such a hard time about my schedule (since school finished he won't give me back my day shifts - that he took away from me in the first place) But everyone else can work regular & come in @ 1:00 - just a bunch of bullshit that he puts me through. So i decied that I'm gonna start dancing in Rhode Island. i found 2 or 3 clubs that i want to check out & then i'm gonna do ametur night & try it out. Hopefully this helps us out. Cuz we definitly need to step it up a noch. i can't take it anymore. so we'll see what happens!

Boxing is great! I love it. It gives me so much energy & the best work out ever. It's such a challenge and it kicks my ass. I'm waiting for an appt @ Mass General for my A.D.D cuz i really feel being in school & dealing w/ everythin else really stresses me out & i feel like i need medication. When i was young, my ma never wanted me on it - which is fine, but now i feel like i need extra help. I'm taking a summer class, hopefully that goes well. I figured if i take that then it will take a load off me for next semester. Life can maybe be a little easier. Well gotta go. Bye.

*Came up = make a lot of money quickly

March 10, 2015

Fighting Back

I was in survival mode and wanted to make enough money so I could finally retire.

My trafficker was promising me that if I just made X amount of dollars I could stop, and we could open a business. I would be graduating the next year, so the pressure was on to save as much money as possible. There was a means to the end, so he said. But the daily hardship of being in the game was obviously taking a toll on me mentally and physically.

Boxing was giving me some freedom and confidence. I remember the day I met my trainer and he saw my black eye. He said that he would teach me how to bob and weave so that

would never happen again. It never did happen again. I was getting tougher and fighting back, fighting for my life.

Many women and girls who are being sex trafficked end up self-medicating by abusing prescription or street drugs. Do I need to explain why? People who aren't being trafficked do the same thing! Please, don't judge those women and girls who you see addicted and on the streets. There's one thing I know: A little girl doesn't dream of becoming a prostitute or an addict. Someone stole her life and sold her a fake dream that turned into a nightmare. I urge you to choose compassion and take action. When one suffers, others suffer.

This letter may come a shock to ya'll because it may seem as if I had no consideration for you all after I left. I really am sorry and I guess that comes to you when you probably could give a flying fuck of my apologies. I really miss you all and I appreciate everything that was given to me and shared with me, and I really hate what I have done. I started to feel guilty as soon as I realized that I couldn't come back. The reason being was of course my daughter. And yes I am sure you would have understood my reasons and would have respected me if I called just to give a reason. I didn't because I felt like I owed ya'll a lot for opening up your family to me and I really felt welcomed and really connected with you and jazz. Jazz you were especially close to me because you knew my grief and you knew how I felt about being new to the whole situation. ■ you treated me with such acceptance and there was never a moment that you doubted my loyalty or let me feel like I wasn't accepted and you also demanded that I be treated with respect by everyone else and for that I will always owe you. I have created a new life here trying to be the best mother I can be, I have a good job (according to the square world). I wish there was a way that I could make things right but at this moment my hands are really tied, I owe a lot more to my child whom has gone through a huge ordeal and I can't give her the type of childhood my mother gave me. This wouldn't be possible if I made a permanent move to Boston. I really thank you for all you acceptance and I wish the best for your family, I know someday ya'll will have everything you hearts desire because you strive to stay focus, that is a lesson I will never forget as I strive to do just that. I learned that maybe If I didn't have a child that really need me all the time we wouldn't be in this situation, but I have a bueatiful daughter that I must set an example for and right now I intend on being the best example. AGAIN thanks, I will never forget you all.

05-21-03

Victoria's letter.

July 25, 2003

B is going to work on his temper & attitude. Even though that same night he told me that he'd be home - but never showed up. So I guess he's saying that he's trying - we'll see. I hope he does. Cuz his attitude is the main reason why I cannot be with him. Another thing we're both gonna work on is the "feelings". We both know we have feelings for each other. - The problem is how they get in the way. One minute we're kissing & the next we're arguing. It's to much. Like B said "we need to put it all in perspective". We know how we feel but put those feelings to the side & "do the god-damn thing". - So hopefully we can work on our issues this time.

I've decied that after I finish school next year, i want to buy a house. Either to live in or rent. if B wants to move in w/ me Ok. If not Ok. We'll see. i just want something of my own. Something that i can say I've worked for & got. It will be 4 yrs next year. Crazy! B also said that he understands & will try to put money away in an account for me - which i hope happens. - But what i need to work on for that to happen is how i work. I need to stay completly focused this whole year. I can't let feelings & other problems get in my way of making money.

Cuz I'm at the point now that i will leave B - no question. So when i leave him. What am i gonna do? go do what I'm doin now? - alone? That's scary a little. Dangerous also. So if i have somebody that is trying to get paid & do good for himself, why not stay and proceed w/ what we set out to do back 3 years ago.? I Just hope it goes as planned & we will succed!

March 17, 2015

Anticipating

I was trapped, but hoping for a better future. Therefore, I was willing to do whatever had to be done to finish and get out of the game. Feeling alone and scared was part of my daily life. Mixed feelings of hating and loving my trafficker at the same time were normal.

In recovery, I have learned that I needed some measure of hope to survive what I was going through.

Waiting for him to change his attitude meant hoping he would stop being violent and oppressive. Hoping he would save money for me meant I had to work more and make him happy. I was hoping, waiting, anxiously anticipating—all for nothing.

When I finally did get away from him, the only place I could find peace and comfort was in drugs and alcohol.

Then, all hope would be lost.

July 26, 2003

Well Today is another crazy day. B & I are going through some serious shit. Let me first start off by saying that i haven't been to the health club in a month cuz we've started this other shit, advertising on the Internet & stayin at hotels. So in the first place - it's hard to be w/ B all the time, never mind when I'm working.

March 19, 2015

You Do Something

Having another crazy day was normal. "Serious shit" meant arguing for hours, violence and more.

The next entry will be a month later, and I will be diagnosing myself with depression and ADD. I could not figure out why I was feeling suicidal and depressed. I never once saw the direct link to what was happening in my life and how it was affecting my health. As I look back, I remember taking antacids every day so the nauseous feeling and constant lump in my throat would go away. No matter how many Tums I took, I never got relief.

My trafficker started using the popular internet website Craigslist and other adult sex sites to post ads of me for sale.

It boggles my mind that you can buy a person and a used fridge on the same website!

He would drive me to the hotels and to the sex buyers' houses when they made appointments. This was difficult because he was with me more often than before. I had to break myself after every client, meaning that I had to hand over all the money right away. I was used to being alone when I worked at the massage parlor in Maine. Since this was new, he wanted to make sure that I was doing what I was supposed to do. Also, there was more risk when prostituting in hotels and at men's houses, not that my trafficker cared what happened to me. But being alone in a hotel room or in a house was an obvious danger. Many women have been assaulted or murdered by sex buyers in these situations because no one knows what's going on behind closed doors. And sadly, no one comes looking for them when they disappear.

Thankfully, I was never assaulted by a sex buyer, but I had my share of really sick men. I will not share the horrible things I have experienced and witnessed, except one vivid memory when I was working at an upscale hotel in Copley Plaza in Boston. The sex buyer came in and we quickly negotiated. Once he left I realized he had given me $250 in fake money. My trafficker wasn't happy. I had to make up for that in more ways than I care to share with you.

Having said that, if you are often in hotels or see something strange happening in your neighborhood, such as lots of people coming and going out of an apartment or business, take a minute to think about what may be going on. If you can do something safely without putting yourself at risk, then do it. Because she is worth it!

August 14, 2003

What I feel: Anxiety. I get more nervous & impaitient lately. I feel (inside) like weird. I feel like this when someone else is driving & we are trying to find something - also when i have alot to do -

school, work, house.. I get overwhelmed. I feel better after a while goes by.

I get headaches sometimes - maybe more than sometimes. I find that "tension" formula works best. I think i am tense. I even get impaitient w/ my electric toothbrush - cuz it is times 30 seconds on each side!! I am irritable, tense, have difficulty concentrating. I have unsatisfying sleep sometimes. I am constipated. I have mood swings - I don't like to think I do, but sometimes I'm happy then the next min - I'm upset @ nothing really. I can't make up my mind. I feel confused, sometimes angry. Sometimes i have a loss of words.

I think i am to organized. I have to be in "total control" or I get nervous or tense. I wash my hands constantly. I pick things up off the ground sometimes cuz i feel like if i don't then something bad might happen. I check things twice, usually. I second guess myself. I feel tired sometimes. I can't sit still for a long time. When i read something i forget it, or while I'm reading like a magazine or newspaper my mind wanders away somewhere.

If i do sit still i will fall asleep. I fell asleep while B was getting a haircut. I fall asleep if i watch TV. I get 6-7 hours of sleep - but i am still tired. When i do homework, i can fall asleep.

When i was on birth control pills i felt crazy. like hormones where everywhere! i was even more jumpy & irritable. I don't like to take them. - when i took the depo shot I got bad headaches.

I feel numb to emotions. Sometimes & then i am to emotional! I tend to think negative. If B tells me he loves me or misses me. I think he's lying. I feel like I am missing out on the really good things in life because i don't allow myself to enjoy them.

I can't seem to put things into perspective well. When i get into a slump - or a normal situation like anyone else - I get upset or sad. But then I can't seem to get out of it. I feel bad and hold on to it. Trying so hard to fix it but I can't, Then i can't even describe when the hell is wrong! Sometimes i have thoughts of killing B or myself.

I seem to get agitated quickly. Then i make a quick choice, well sometimes I get confused. I work on impulse. I make people pick for me cuz i can't make up my mind. Sometimes I'm happy and sometimes I'm sad. I'm sick of it. I've read books - Well i've tried but i feel like nothing happens cuz i can't even concentrate while reading it!

I have done yoga but seem to have lost interest in that. I like pilates better cuz it's faster. I work out like a nut. I work out very hard. I try to eat good but then I seem not to care and eat whatever I want. I like big portions. I love sweets and chocolate. But then sometimes I have eaten so much that i feel like i have to throw up - and sometimes I do. Either I make myself or it happens. Then since i've thrown up so much, I can't go to the bathroom correctly.

So if i am depressed, is it cuz i have ADD or do i feel anxiety cuz of my ADD? I'm just depressed, is that why I have all these problems? I've used drugs & sometimes i can use to much. i used to drink hard liquor - from age 14 to 20. That was bad. Now when i drink to much or fast i get terrible pains in my stomach. I don't drink as much anymore but when I was prescribed pain pills i liked to take them. That was recently. I didn't take them often so I spread it out, so when I really felt stressed I would have them cuz I didn't have a refill.

I wash my hands alot. I check doors, pick up things. I am overly organized. Everything has a place. I hold on to items for a while. Then force myself to get rid of them later. I repeat things in my head all of the time. I feel fear - like if I don't do something then something bad will happen. I think about getting dieases and fear them. Like AIDS or Cancer?!! & then when i think of them i do the sign of the cross. Sometimes 2 when i drive by a church. I pray every night before I sleep & i say the same exact thing. I have to beep twice when i leave somewhere (like my mothers espcially) I clean everything in my house every sunday & if I don't then i feel unsatisfied. I skeeve anything & everything. If B has dirty hands, which i think he does all of the time, then i get grossed out & don't even want him to touch me until I see him wash them.

When I took the Adderall I immediately felt different. My heart felt like it was going faster, my eyes felt wide and I had dry mouth. I clenched my teeth all day. I drank so much water. My stomach felt weird, like I had to go the bathroom. I felt nervous, then Ok. I didn't eat much and ate a small dinner. I worked out and then felt Ok. But i just don't like to take things that make me feel like "not me". i don't like to feel weird.

I felt like i needed to find a better solution then this medicine. So i went online & found out a hole lot of info on myself that was inside of me lurking around. I feel so much better, it's 4 am & I'm still up. I can't sleep cuz I'm thinking so much. So it helped me in some ways & made me feel bad inside, like my heart beating so fast was the worst. I felt so jittery.

March 24, 2015

Anti-slavery

The definition for the word freedom is: "the quality or state of being free; the absence of necessity, coercion, or constraint in choice or action; liberation from slavery or restraint or from the power of another; independence".

My diary entry was far from that definition. As I reread it, I see that I was a young and vulnerable girl who was being held prisoner in her own body.

When I share my story of surviving sex trafficking, I want the audience to get a clear picture of what was going on and why I stayed for five years. I wasn't handcuffed to a radiator like some people might imagine. Rather, I was mentally and emotionally held captive. I was living under severe oppression, and my emotions were either all over the place or shut off. Thoughts of suicide and homicide were common. Self-medicating was bound to happen.

Right now, millions of women and girls are dealing with more complex issues than I was. It is my hope that you can understand the mind frame of a victim because of that entry. I hope it helps you understand the complexity of this supposedly victim-less crime.

My recovery has been very difficult. There have been many moments when I've wanted to forget it and go back to the streets. I remind myself that going back is not an option.

I recall everything I have to be thankful for. I remember that I have been set free by my Liberating King! Most important, I am fighting for my continued freedom and the freedom for others.

Isaiah 61:1 states:

"The Spirit of the Lord, the Eternal, is on me.

The Lord has appointed me for a special purpose.

He has anointed me to bring good news to the poor.

He has sent me to repair broken hearts,

And to declare to those who are held captive and bound in prison—be free from your imprisonment!"

October 22, 2003

Ok. Well today is the 22nd of Oct, & I'm @ my mothers. Wow huh? I've been here since thursday the 16th . Something inside of my mind clicked & finally stuck. - I've had enough. I told myself that i was never gonna pay this man again. & i moved out what i could on thurs & on friday my father & I moved EVERYTHING out. It was the hardest thing ever. i felt soo bad cuz he was there as i was moving. - Maggie came & they left so he'd calm down. I cried and cried.

March 31, 2015

Hidden Persistence

I bet you're thinking this is fantastic news and that the next entry will be about me putting my life back together. Sadly, the answer is NO.

I would like to say that this was the last time I was leaving, that it was easy. But it wasn't. I don't remember how many

times I moved out of my trafficker's house because it's too many to count.

December 25, 2003!

Well Merry Christmas! :) I've been out of the house of evil for 2 months! - Actually more! I'm so happy being home & away from him. Today is Christmas day & I feel well OK - my mom's back was really hurting her & the medicine they gave her - gave her a bad rash - so now she's not feeling to good. We usually open gifts early, but not this year. It just seems like everyone is stressed. My aunt, non & Chris is here - making it harder. But all i can do is take deep breaths & take it easy. At times i get anxiety - i can feel it. But i don't let it show. I just say "whatever". It's funny how as i write my handwritting changes because my hand hurts.

Ok SO Adam came by last night & i gave him a gift. He said he liked it. I got him sweat pants and a thermal style shirt cuz i never see him anything but a tie. He gave me 12 beautiful pink roses & a very nice card. :) He makes me happy. He also said that he got me something else but it's on the way. I can't wait! We're going to Florida Jan 11th. That should be a lot of fun. Just him & i spending days together. Doing nothing is Ok. He brings peace when he's around. Nothing else seems to matter. I've never felt like this before. I like it. He's coming over later. We plan to talk about where we stand in our relationship. We both know that we like each other. The other night he said that he loved me & cared a lot about me. Then went on & asked if I <3 him like a boyfriend? I said - Not right now - but it will grow. He said he loves me more than a brother loves a sister - I think he's just going crazy w/ all the thoughts, feelings & emotions running through his mind & body. It's like our realtionship has moved & evolved but not to fast. I think it's going at a pace it's supposed to. We met for a "real reason". I know we did.

No matter how bad my life was w/ B & I moved to Everett, who did I meet? Adam at the grocery store! From the first day i saw him - walking down one of the aisle's, we made eye contact - & then every time there after. I would look for him when i went in there. I'd see him and I'd smile at him. I'd have his attention & butterflies in my stomach. He'd smile back & look at me w/ his body language telling me to come talk to him. It was like slow motion. - Meanwhile I was having a heart attack! And I'd be on the phone with my ma - Dying!! Being all gitty. Then after a while we introduced ourselves - I'd have dreams about him, wake up and be like damn! B would be home, next to me - or out - and I'd always think of Adam.

I've made it through a tough time - Adam accepted me - for me & my past. I remember being so worried after i told him - i thought for sure he was going to say the hell w/ her & her drama - But nope. He's still here. Like "I'm still here." I don't think, Well I do think - that he respects me for telling him & being so real about it. He knows understands how shitty it's been for me & he knows we all make decisions in life that we're not proud of. He knows that no-one's perfect. I know he has questions - about what life was like for me. He asked if I ever wore wigs?! I laughed and told him - no, never. It was just me. - Then he made a comment like I was on the street, but in a joking way - and I said no, no, I wasn't there I was in a house... I don't mind if he asks - but I just don't want him to laugh or make jokes. - Even though i know he's just doing it cuz he probably feels uncomfortable. -

*So i gotta go open gifts. Yay. ♥Love, Peace & :) happiness *always* Jazz*

April 2, 2015

Grocery Store

Adam was a sweetheart and at the same time he was naive. He worked at the same grocery store where I shopped. My trafficker had no idea about this other man. If he had known, I would not be writing about it. I'd be dead. I would also like to say that this time away from the house of evil was my last escape. But it wasn't. As we know, relapse is a part of the process. Shortly after having some freedom, I would go back to what was *familiar*—oppression, abuse, and violence.

Breaking free was the most difficult thing I have ever done because I believed all the lies. I believed I was a no good dirty ho. They said, "You can never make a ho a housewife." Therefore, I believed I never would be anything more. Even though I desperately wanted to live a normal, safe and healthy life, I just didn't know how to do it. The relationship between Adam and me would end before I went back to my trafficker. I don't even remember how it ended. It just did. Like most of the dreams I had, this one just faded away.

Editor's Note:

In a study published in the June 2016 online journal *eLife*, research suggested that empathy is not an automatic or instinctive process, but rather a deliberate process that involves "taking another person's perspective"—particularly, imagining another person's thoughts and intentions.

Tor Wager and his team reported that the ability to understand and empathize with another person's pain is based on complex brain interactions. The results raise questions about ways to help people relate to others when they feel physical or emotional pain.

Published in *The Journal of Positive Psychology* in May 2014, a study done by Baylor University researcher Thomas Carpenter showed that it's easier to forgive ourselves for hurting someone if we first make amends with them. The study showed that the more people made amends, the more they believed self-forgiveness was morally permissible.

Also in May 2014, another study was published *Psychological Science.* Researchers Malcolm MacLeod and Raynette Bierman found that after a transgression had been forgiven, then forgetting about the transgression seemed to become easier.

Chapter 5

Diary: Year 2004

January 4, 03 - oops - 2004!

New years is a time that everyone says that they want to start something new. - Bring the new year in correct & keep your word. My new years "agreement" w/ myself is to stay completly focused on what I'm doing & be in total control of what's going on in my life at all times. I'm going to have my own goals & promises to myself. No-one else is going to be able to influence my thoughts & No - one should have ever.

I'm very proud - looking back - of how I came through. I really did step out of a messed up situation & did it w/ grace. I was totally stressed & my mind was filled w/ negative thoughts & hate. Now I will & I am clearing my mind & will fill it w/ positive & hopeful feelings. "No more drama - No more fear". - "Forever Free" Free myself from everything negative & wrong - everything that tears me down or has in my past.

Priorities First. Keep Focused. -

1) Get personal trainer certificate going!

2) Do good in school. Almost done!

3) Compete in Fitness pagent in April! Do the best I can.

4) Take fitness to the next level & fitness model.

5) Definitely move! Cali/NY? Gotta get out of Saugus. Like Adam said "Girl, you're to big for Saugus!"

6) Live healthy, eat clean & workout, get sleep

7) Stay focused!! Don't forget.

April 7, 2015

Getting Healthy

The entry before this one was in December, and I had moved home to my parents' house. The next month, in January, I had gone back to my trafficker. This time, I made a vow to myself to always have total control of my life. My life was so out of my control and trying to control it would make me feel normal. I broke up with Adam and went back to the game—and to B, my trafficker—because it was all I knew how to do. I remember thinking that things would be different this time.

Since I had been boxing, I really got into my health and working out. I weighed a lean 118 pounds and was a size 0 at one point. I became obsessed with my body and the way I looked. Again, I was controlling what I could. I found fitness pageants and thought that becoming a fitness model and personal trainer was a great idea. I thought I could travel around, compete and work as a high-priced escort. This would make us a lot more money. Also, I took dance as a child, so I enjoyed this aspect of it.

This idea wouldn't last long, as my trafficker didn't allow me to continue working out or competing. I loved the self-esteem boost that working out was giving me. I found freedom in riding my bike to the studio and working out hard. But once again, my dreams faded. It began when he stopped by the gym where I was training and got into a fight with my personal trainer. Soon I had to stop working out there. Any time I would gain some freedom or self-worth, B was right there, quickly stealing it away.

Now when I look back, I see the fitness model industry as a gateway to exploitation. Those pictures of me don't show my fitness abilities, rather something more suggestive. But at least I had my clothes on.

Fitness photos.

(These are random notes without a date.)

i think my world is soo crazy. My world. Meaning my life, my everyday. B isn't the man that i would want to be w/ because, he is not the one i believe if [is] for me. I know he cares for me, as i care for him. But he seems so grown & at times he seems so young. I *know he will succeed, somehow.. I know he has dreams.. Dreams that are realistic. He doesn't want to be broke, or bummy 4 life. His actions just make me nervous. Maybe cuz i don't feel stable. I - we live day to day. I never know how much I'll make for a week, it's a guess, it's a chance, just hoping there's business & enough to make $.*

As a boyfriend, NO. - No way - he pisses me off so bad, he still talks to his old girlfriend on the reg. He doesn't come home at night a lot of the times. In business, he pisses me off cuz he still f*cks w/ Maggie & she doesn't work... How messed up is that. I'm goin to school, workin 4 days bustin my ass & this bitch is still around. I really don't get it. He be talkin to mad chicks, where are they? None of them are down right now. He isn't sincere. He can be real about making money & Hustlin but love - Na. I hate how lazy he can be. From smoking so much weed to not taking out the trash. I just don't know. I mean the only time I saw something good happening was when we stacked $18,000. He let me stack all that. It was when the two other chics were around. Then X-mas came & poof. Gone. all $18Gs. Just like that.. Easy come. Easy go.

Now it's just me & him hustlin, He's stressed.. I'm fed up & he know's when J gets bored or J feels like she's not succeeding the way she wants, J wanders - mind & body. Look what happened before. If I don't feel good w/ B, then I'll go somewhere else or start being shady. But that's not what I'm gonna do this time. I won't go out like that. Cuz he doesn't understand fully. I'm gonna be patient and finish school. & wait.

Hopefully - B will come through & be the man that he thinks he is. He said the other day.. When we were talking or arguing - I can't remember. He said, "What am i gonna do when it's time for you & i don't have any money? Nothing to give you? You'll think I'm fucked up right??!" & So right then i realized that he knows that i don't want to be w/ him 4-ever. & That he wants to best 4 me later in life. & He wants to give me what i want, He is good to me in that way & he insists that that is why he is such a good man. But he doesn't realize that all that other shit he pulls - pisses me off. Soo much that i can't stand being with him. It's to bad.How i really feel

Love, B - Work. Pregnancy. - Relationship. Life.

I love B as my first real man. First real relationship & life changing experience. I feel that i cannot fully be myself w/ B. I've always felt that way. We've had some issues, my fault & his. But that's not the blame. I've grown away. I feel different. After the pregnancy & how he handled it. I changed my feelings.

I moved out. And came back. Told him to give me X amount of $ a week. So I feel more independent & can pay my own way. - That still isn't enough. He's tried, I know he has. I appreciate that & I am glad that he's been as understanding as he's been. - Which he's really tried to understand me. I just know that he is not the one & my time has come. I need to move on. 5 years of craziness, crying, fighting, hitting, yelling, resenting, fearing, loving, hating, cheating - lying..

I feel like he cheats or is not as honest as he should be. He sleeps out - stays out for hours - when he comes back. I ask no questions & sneak a peak @ his phone to play detecive... Not good because all i do is make it worse for myself. not knowing what he's doing. To afraid to ask. & allowing myself to assume the worst. - It makes me feel horrible. - So i put up a shield & try not to care.

That & other things mess w/ my mind. I can't even enjoy sex w/ him. because of that, the pregnancy & i think that work also makes me hate doing it. I hate the way i feel, I hate when a guy touches me, half the time i feel nauseous, sick & when I'm w/ B the last thing i want is to have sex. Even though work doesn't feel like B & i don't enjoy it - But i used to w/ B. Now i feel like oh my God - what if I become pregnant again. We don't like to use condoms. I try but he doesn't like them. I feel like he uses them w/ other girls.

I hate this - This game has torn me apart & ruined what could have been the greatest love of my life & B's. It's making me cry to write this, But i guess i needed it.

I just want to be alone to find out who i really am & what i want in life. I can't stand to be in this situation any longer. It hurts to bad & makes me sad. B doesn't deserve that. I'm always snappy, unhappy & bitchy. He can't even get sex. - The only reason why i came back was because i felt like i had no choice. Money is what makes the world go around. & that's all i know now. Square jobs wasn't making me happy. So i went back.. got pregnant.. He didn't think itt was a good time. I think about what it would have been like to be pregnant right now.. I'd be 6 months pregnant. What would it have been? Names? Looked like? I get soo sad when I think about it.-- It really hurts.

I thought B would of wanted it just as much as me. All I've done for him --- Sacrificed, Risked, and he makes a baby with me.. Then he's not ready. Now i have to live w/ another shitty memory.. For the rest of my life.. What it takes to be a woman - only a woman can understand. The shit we put up w/. with a man.

I've become stronger, wiser & better as I've grown & thanks to B & the game.

I'll never go home.

I'm hurting inside & can't stop thinking of what life could be like w/out this misery. How to be happy w/ myself? What makes me happy? But being alone. I've been unhappy - & sad, still working, making money - paying bills, cooking, cleaning... I keep going to keep me busy. So i don't have time to sit & think.. Cuz when i think - i cry., I get scared & don't know what to say.

Just let me live my life. I've given u all I can.. Please B please understand.

I've loved you & gave you my all. Every step of the way... I'll never forget what you've done.. or what you've made me into.. It's been soo hard.. I just can't do it anymore.

April 21, 2015

The Exit

That has been one of the most difficult entries to read. When I began to reflect on it, I had to stop because of the emotional pain. It brought lots of healing tears. All the memories came flooding back; it was too much for me to process at once.

In my mind, I was in that place—that young girl, sitting in my bedroom, writing on a tear-soaked notebook and grieving the loss of a baby. I had no say or control over what was happening to my own body.

I knew if I didn't go to the abortion clinic, he was going to hurt me in such a way that I would lose the baby. I remember being at Planned Parenthood and feeling too scared to tell anyone what was going on in my life. They had no clue I was a trafficking victim, but neither did I.

This is the sad reality of sex trafficking in America. Our daughters are out there—being forced by fists, weapons, poverty, drugs or the pursuit of love to do things with their bodies that they never imagined. And they don't see a way out.

How I escaped for the last time is nothing but a divine intervention in my life. Let me explain. While I was with my trafficker, I developed a friendship with a sex buyer. I'll call him Vinny. He was contacting me from an ad he saw on an escort website. Every time I visited him at his house, we just talked for hours, and he paid me good money. He never touched me. This was not something that I was used to. Somewhere in the back of my mind, I must have considered him to be safe.

At the same time, I was saving money without my trafficker knowing about it. I would take a few hundred dollars off the top of what I made for that day, put it in a ziploc baggie, tie elastics around it and hide it in the dirt in my large potted plants. I did this for a few months and when I saved a few thousand dollars, I wanted to get my own apartment.

But how does a victim of sex trafficking fill out a rental application that requires her to have a job, references, a back ground check and so on? Never mind that she has trauma, mental illness, substance abuse issues, a criminal record and children to support. All those real issues make the exit much more unattainable.

I felt trapped, but I was determined to get out. I decided to email Vinny and ask him for help. He owned a small business, and I asked him if I could lie on my rental application and say that I worked for him as a bookkeeper. He agreed, and I got the apartment.

On the day I was moving out, I packed up a few things in trash bags. Then I called the local police and asked them to come over and wait on the porch, so my boyfriend wouldn't get violent when I moved out. They did just that. And B made sure to tell me on the way out the door, "God don't like ugly, and you will pay for this." I took a deep breath, put my cat and dog in one of the cars that I had in my name and drove off.

Editor's Note:

Researcher E.S. Rosenzweig reported in the journal *Nature Neuroscience* in 2002 that when the brain unlearns something, the connections between neurons go through a chemical process called long-term synaptic depression. This chemical process weakens the connections between neurons.

Although oxytocin helps to build commitment and bonding, it can also build new brain connections. Neuroscientist Walter J. Freeman suggests from his research published in the journal *Nature Neuroscience* in 2003 that oxytocin not only forms brain connections, but also it can melt old brain connections so that new connections and new learning can occur. Also, because oxytocin is a feel-good chemical, it may reduce stress so learning becomes easier.

Chapter 6

Diary: Year 2005

January 25, 2005

Wow. Well I am @ work. Real Work. It feels good to be here. I don't mind it @ all. I'm doing good. I feel it as I speak. A sense of happiness & calmness. Alot has happend & gone on in the past months. Therepy has helped soo much. Travis is wonderful. Sometimes lately I have been getting the urge to make money because I don't have any. & I know that rent is due, & everything else. But I've talked to Travis about it & he said that he will help me, through it. I want to keep working. I will even get second night job - waitressing... anything to help. It really feels good to have a job & Travis. I am looking 4 a better paying job.. But 4 now I am ok.

It means alot to have self respect, dignity & pride. Travis is helping me realize that I can have a normal realtionship w/ love & caring.. not money as the ruler. I just hope it all works out.. I am planning on going to UMass this fall. I definitly need to do that for myself. I just have the disipline & want to succeed & get a Bachelors degree. It means alot even if I'll be 27, getting it! I still did it. So as I sit here @ my reception desk. I sigh & look towards a brighter & better (positive) future. Lets hope. Love Me.

April 23, 2015

Choices

Getting out of sex trafficking and starting a new life is one of the most difficult things I have done. I didn't have a "safe home" or program to go to. I had to pay $1,200 for rent, $600 for a car payment and other debt that I unwillingly acquired while being trafficked.

I found a therapist from Victims of Violence. Although she really didn't understand my trauma or life experience, she did help me until I started abusing the powerful pain medication Oxycontin. Getting high and numbing the pain was much better than recounting all of my trauma to someone who, I believe, didn't get it.

This is the reality for most women getting out of prostitution or the sex industry. They will most likely go back to what they know, unless their basic needs are met in a way that empowers them and gives them self-worth. This did not happen for me and, sadly, it doesn't happen for many others because of the lack of understanding, funding and resources.

Just now, I had the amazing realization that I never did attend the University of Massachusetts that fall as I had planned. Rather, at the age of 27, I was in and out of detoxes trying to get off heroin. Yes, I was the junkie that was overdosing in the bathrooms at Dunkin' Donuts and would have stolen your wallet if I had the chance.

Still, today is a day for me to celebrate. I have come a long way, and I still have a long way to go. But I am beyond blessed. Today I have a choice about where I want my life to go and how to get there.

February 1, 2005

Let me take a minute & write. That sounds good. I have soo much going on right now... Way to much to think about, Well I am *thinking but not clearly.*

1.) Travis: I really do like him, But not enough to want to stay.

2.) Money: I like working a Reg. Job.

2A.) Work: I need to make money to pay my bills.

3.) Car: I like the car, but it's to expensive.

1.) When i am w/ him i feel soo good.. Soo much like i want to tell him that i love him. But when I am not w/ him I don't feel any different.. Like I don't care. Basically I just don't think that I am or want a boyfriend @ this time. I was all set when i met him. I didn't even want to talk to him - that's why he chased me. Then I gave in & let my heart go - I talked to him and told him everything. He accepted. But I realize that I'm just not able to be "me" around him.

I still want to work.. About work. I would like to - I am just not ready to completely stop working. I mean - lets face it. I have been working for all these years. I am now @ a regular job - which is great. I like it here. It's just that I want that extra money on the side. I want to pay off my credit card bills. I want to go to school in the fall & be able to pay the way (at least some of it).. W/ Travis around - it just stops me from being able to live free like I want to. I just don't want any restrictions. I like to party and hang out. - I mean I just really don't want to hide myself around a man - my boyfriend. or anyone.

I feel like I have my own personal things I need to handle. Like I was just in a long abusive realtionship.. I need time to get back to me.. Who am I? Where am i going? What do i want to do? Being around Travis has helped give me the push I need to get started. He helped me realize that someone can have real feelings for me. That I am lovable, no matter what I've done in my past. I have a regular job & I actually like it. I do. I like coming to work. I just need that extra side money & space to be able to do what I want. Wheather it be work, party.. etc..

April 28, 2015

Pain Medication

I was facing a dilemma. I was out from under the grips of my pimp, but I couldn't fully support myself financially. This is very common for most girls and women exiting sex trafficking. It's one of the reasons we go back into the game. We return to our trafficker because of the intense trauma bonds or the lack of money and other resources we need to make a successful exit.

I was also starting to drink and party often. I was hanging out with new and old friends, and they were all getting high off Oxycontin. This was at a time when the pills, Oxy 80's, were in high demand and easily obtained in my area.

I didn't realize that I would become addicted. I didn't know that I was numbing the emotional pain. I didn't know that I was running away from myself. All I knew was that I felt better high, than not high.

Travis wasn't into that scene. He was cramping my style. So what does a girl do? She breaks up with him and gets into a relationship with the drug dealer.

The growing drug addiction mixed with other events and life pressures would force me back into the life of prostitution. Researchers call this survival sex or survival prostitution. A trafficker would call me a renegade.

You can learn more about survival prostitution and other research done by Melissa Farley, a leading researcher in the field. Visit her website at: ProstitutionReasearch.com.

February 7, 2005

Hi Ok I am writing again.. So what a week. I broke up w/ Travis & he came by yesterday.. and I end up telling him "I love U" I was full of emotions and crying. I just couldn't help it. I know I like him.

But last week was hard for me. & I needed money. - So i did what i had to do.

But this week is different. I don't want to do the OC's anymore. I had enough of that. & i really don't think I want anyone to move in. The only reason why I would want someone to move in would be to lower the rent. Maybe I will move in with T. I think it would be good & I do want to be normal and in a healthy relationship. I am ready to be close to him. I just couldn't pay my bills. (the rent). & It freaked me out.

So I know what to do to make money - & that's what I did. I didn't have the heart to do it while being with him. Plus I let doing that, doing drugs and my friends influence me into letting him go. Which was wrong. I need to re-evaluate what's happening. And how I want to live my life. Partying isn't all that fun. This weekend I was really up till 6am. & it was pointless. I spent money that i needed - & felt like shit. What is the point of that? When i could have spent it w/ Travis & had a good time w/out drugs & not until 6am.

It's weird cuz at IOP, the therapist said to me - "So when are you gonna fully retire? - What about a boyfriend?" "By doing this, you're not allowing yourself to have a boyfriend". I was like, whatever - and kind of blew it off. But he was right. I am not allowing anything. I am sooo money driven by the money that I almost don't care about anything else. I don't care about myself, pride, dignity or self worth. I am allowing the game to control me. Yeah - so what I have credit card bills, and I want to pay them off. I will over time. I have a car note and insurance. I have to get rid of this car & my finances will be ok. I will work hard & may not be rich - but will be happy living w/ T & having someone genuinly love me for me.

I am just so used to having to make the money. I can't just sit down & chill. I always have to be moving. That's how it was. I had to take care of everything. Me, B, the house.. Bla bla.

Now i can just chill. work, go to school in the fall & look ahead to my future. - growing, learning to love my self no matter what.

About Travis, he really is awesome. Him being gone for those days really made me wonder & I did think about him. But I've learned to just shut off. When he left my house that evening. well morning.. I just turned off. I acted like it didn't matter... & i tried to move on. Then I saw him yesterday and we kissed and I cried. It was like I was "turned on" or alive. All these feelings that i just don't know what to do w/. I let go... & before you know it, I said I love you. Then we spent the rest of the day together. And now we are gonna move in together. I just have to get my mind right & realize that he loves me and I deserve to be loved. I feel better that I wrote.

May 12, 2015

The Real World

I was fresh out of the life of sex trafficking and learning how to do life on life's terms. It is not for the faint of heart. I was struggling to pay my bills and working a square job as a secretary was not providing enough income. That is what pushed me back into prostitution.

Realize this: I was trying to survive in the real world with a huge amount of trauma and a growing drug addiction. At the same time, I was in therapy and attending intensive out-patient sessions on a weekly basis. Why the therapist thought I needed to fully retire, so I could get a boyfriend is beyond me. A boyfriend was the last thing I needed. What I needed was some skills for coping and a safe place to talk about my experiences without being told what to do or being judged.

I was like a fish out of water experiencing feelings and emotions that I had numbed or shut off for so long. In addition to using Oxycontin, I was using cocaine. This was bad and good. It was good because it numbed the emotional pain and anxiety I was feeling. It was bad because you can't live life successfully and do drugs. I know this. I've tried it.

This was just the beginning of a long, slow ride to hell. I would soon be fully addicted and endure more trauma, abuse and prostitution.

What if there had been a house—a safe haven, where I could have lived rent free for a year or two while I got my life back on track? Currently, there is a severe shortage of safe housing for women who want to exit sex trafficking. Many efforts are being made to open safe homes and develop programs for survivors, and that is awesome.

However, we simply need more attention focused on this issue and more funding to sustain these programs. If we want to make a difference in the anti-trafficking movement, I believe it takes the whole community to prevent exploitation and trafficking and to provide aftercare for survivors.

In 2014, I was honored to share my voice and thoughts on this issue in an article that I wrote for one of the country's well-known, anti-trafficking organizations Truckers Against Trafficking. You can visit their website to learn more: www.TruckersAgainstTrafficking.org

---

February 10, 2005

Well what a day. It's been Ok. & I feel Ok. Tonight I am going to Salon 45 to see Maria & cut Kasey's hair for a demo. I might work there part time. But a guy I work with at the printing company's brother own's a nightclub in Boston & I might be able to cocktail waitress there too.. SO I'm not sure yet. But I definitly need that extra money. I'm not sure if Kasey is going to move in or not. I might have to move out. But I doubt that I can find a cheaper place.

So last night I wanted to call B. But i don't have his new cell number. Something inside me - wants to talk. See & be with him. Why I have no idea. All that we've been through... & So today i call his store & Maggie answers. I hung up before she answered though - So she calls back & says "Jazz if ur gonna call here don't hang up when i answer". And I told her that I didn't even know she picked up - Cuz i hung up before i even heard her voice. I get all pissed & felt the inside of me boiling. I was angry & i remembered the way i used to feel about her.

I finally spoke to B later on today & told him. He said she already told him that i called.. but not about what happened about her calling me back.

May 21, 2015

Advocate

Yes, I called my trafficker after I was free from him. Why? Because relapse is part of recovery. I didn't know how to live life without him because I lived as his slave for five years. Harriet Tubman, who was born an African-American slave and later became an abolitionist, once said "I freed a thousand slaves. I could have freed a thousand more if only they knew they were slaves."

In my recovery, therapists have educated me about the psychological hold my trafficker had over me, commonly referred to as Stockholm syndrome or trauma bonding. Even though I was abused mentally, emotionally, physically and sexually by my trafficker, I had intense feelings for him. As you read in my previous journal entries, I was in love with him. Secondly, I was struggling financially. I couldn't pay my bills by working a regular 9 to 5 job.

Today, I serve as an advocate and mentor, and I have spoken to many women who have exited sex trafficking. One common thread they share is the lack of money after the exit. Because of that reality, going back to a pimp or the streets seems better than being dead-ass broke. So broke that they can't even buy a bus pass. They are willing to endure more pain to have their basic needs met.

Want to be part of the solution? If you are a business owner and are able to employ women at this stage of recovery, please do it. But please do it without judgment. Many women may come with a criminal record or drug history. Give them a chance and treat them with respect and dignity.

Are you an entrepreneur? Then create meaningful work and products for women so they have a chance at success. Are

you blessed financially? Then donate to safe homes and survivor recovery programs or start a scholarship fund for survivors to further their education.

They are counting on you and the community to empower them and lift them up.

February 15, 2005

Things to always Remember:

- It's not about where you've been, but where your at in this moment.

- Live w/out Regrets Because you live & learn.

- It's better to love atleast once, then not at all.

- God doesn't give you anything that you can't handle.

- You are where your supposed to be @ this very moment.

- Remember yesterday but live for today, the future isn't always promised.

- love, accept & Respect yourself.

What i want to do. Ok I am going to that night club 2-morrow night & from there I will find out my schedule & maybe work @ the salon mon-weds. 10-7 & thurs - sat @ the club. Plus do what i do, on the side. If she pays 50% commission at the salon- then it might be good. But i have to see what happens @ the club first. like how much will i work on an average and what will i make?

I can't wait to go to the "Red string event" @ Harvard law school, thurs night. It will be soo cool to learn all about the Kabbalah & how it works. I am excited.

And B called me a few times yesterday. He called me while I was at dinner w/ Travis but then he didn't call back... So i called him today @ the store & Maggie answered with a slight attitude when i told her to tell him to call me. haha i love it. I am gonna call to see how to get the restraining order taken off. Which i just did. So it looks like I'll have to come to work late one of these days. - I just feel like i should take it off. He has left me alone & respected me. I know this sounds crazy but i feel like i made that decision to get one very quickly & did it because I felt I had no way out. That it was the only way he would leave me alone.. & guess what. It worked but i also pushed him. far . far away. Which is sad. Because yeah, we had a crazy relationship.

It was very difficult, & abusive @ times. But i genuinly loved him & he loved me. That's real. I couldn't deal w/all he put me through. The girls, the work, all the money, the house. Nothing he said meant anything to me after awhile. I began to not know myself. I was lost in this other world that I had taken on. So much was going on. & when you make fast money - life goes by even faster. All those years we were together - flew by. It seems like yesterday. I can remember when I first told him that i loved him & when he told me.

Then i can remember when he put his hands on me. How it was the beginning of the end. life takes on a new meaning when someone you love - someone your partners w/. Abuses you. You begin to survive, not live. Whatevers good for the moment is what matters. Cuz you don't care about tomorrow like you should.

That's what i am in the process of doing now. I am caring about myself & getting my mind right. life is hard to figure out. but being happy w/ yourself can get you through it. To look in the mirror & say - positive things about myself - & really feeling them... That's

June 2, 2015

Trying to Figure Out Life

I was walking around completely traumatized. The way I experienced life was similar to looking through broken lenses. I was a fish out of water. And I was losing air. But I was still fighting for life.

I thought I might find meaning in Kabbalah because Madonna was my idol growing up. As a Jewish convert, she now wears a red string around her wrist. So I thought it might work for me, too. I was searching for meaning and wholeness.

And why would I want to take off the restraining order? Guilt and shame, that's why. I knew I couldn't pay my bills by working a regular 9 to 5 job. So I thought I'd work two jobs and then prostitute on the side. Who prostitutes on the side? Like it's a part-time job or something?! I knew if I was caught prostituting by my former trafficker or another one, that I would be in trouble. So I was trying to make it all work out. I was surviving.

Think about it: I had been trafficked for five years. I had no clue how to do life. I genuinely loved and cared about the man who violated every aspect of the former me. From 19 years old until 24 years old, I was his property. It wasn't that easy to just leave the game. He now owned a store that he was using as his front for all the money he was making off the backs of women. I saw that as ambitious and good.

It would eventually end between us. After I finally broke free for the final time in 2005, I didn't take off the restraining order. He just ended up leaving me alone. I think it was actually by the grace of God.

As time went on, my drug addiction brought me to unimaginable places, and I hit rock bottom. At first, I was abusing Oxycontin on the weekends. Then the weekend started on Thursday. Before I knew it, all the days blended together. I was using every day. I got involved in unhealthy relationships, sold drugs and then got swallowed up and spit out by a growing drug addiction. My life spiraled out of control for the next two years.

Today, I am in the recovery process and fighting for a better life. This time, it's even more important because it's not only for me, but also for every other person out there who has been trafficked or who is vulnerable to trafficking.

October 2005

Just a little notebook to write feelings, thoughts or emotions.

All to help "empower" me.

To Help me become the woman I know I am - Deep inside.

Today is the first day in a long time that I have had the urge to write in a journal. B has finally lost his control over me. In his eyes anyway. I know that it will be a long road for me to truley be over what he has helped me become.

I used to write in a journal when I was feeling blue/lonely/sad/helpless..etc.. now i want to use a journal to write good thoughts. Happy & funny thoughts. I am tired of feeling so depressed & sad. My life for the last 4 1/2 years has been full of hate, regrets, embrassememnt, hurt & fear. My self esteem has gone out the window, my pride & dignity right along with it.

I'll be writting often. Writting is like a therapy & that's definitly what i need. Right now. Please keep strong & hold my head up. J

Things that I know are true

I am single!!

I am pretty

I am friendly

I am honest

I am a good friend

I am good at crocheting

I am good at haircutting

I am good at laughing!!

I am fun

I am open to new ideas

I am worth more Than he gave me.

- What is important to me <3

Friendship, love, caring, honesty, giving, reality, truth, family, My dogs and cat.

I also love my mom! What would i do w/out her? I love her more than anything. She still loves me. I thought she would disown me & hate me. But she didn't. That means more to me than the world.

June 9, 2015

Moments of Clarity

That was the first time I wrote in my journal in eight months. I was feeling more positive, but the journey would become increasingly harder. The reason I was not writing as often was because I was drinking and getting high.

I wanted to live a successful life and experience feelings, but this was scary at times because I had no coping skills. Yet, I had moments of clarity. They were like threads that wove my mistakes and strengths into a beautiful mosaic in my early recovery.

Survivors of sex trafficking are very resilient. We have endured such horrific abuse to our whole being, yet once we leave that life and realize that we are free, this propels us to discover more about the treasures we hold within. We learn what we were originally designed for. It is a slow process. If you are working with survivors who have just exited, please be gentle and patient.

If you are a survivor reading this, may you run free! Go as quickly or slowly as you want. You are in charge of your recovery! Just know that what has happened to you does NOT determine who you are. You have been created for a purpose. There are plans for your life and your pain.

I can promise you this: Nothing goes to waste in God's Kingdom. In the Bible, Jesus says, "Come to Me, all who are weary and burdened, and I will give you rest. Put My yoke upon your shoulders. It might appear heavy at first, but it is perfectly fitted to your curves. Learn from Me, for I am gentle and humble of heart. When you are yoked to Me, your weary souls will find rest. For My yoke is easy, and My burden is light." (Matthew 11:28-30)

Another promise that you can bank on is found in Jeremiah 29:11. "I know the plans I have for you," says the Eternal, "plans for peace, not evil, to give you a future and hope."

Never forget that.

Editor's Note

In an article published in the November 3, 2015 online issue of the journal of *Social Cognitive and Affective Neuroscience*, researchers Christopher Cascio and his team used brain scans to help explain why self-affirmations and self-awareness of personal values can be beneficial.

In their research, the scans of sedentary and overweight participants who repeated self-affirmations showed more activity in the brain areas associated with expecting and receiving rewards—the ventral striatum and the ventral medial prefrontal cortex.

In follow up research during the next month, the participants who performed self-affirmations about positive health messages responded better—as measured by wrist-worn accelerometers—than control participants who did not perform the self-affirmations.

Chapter 7

Diary: Year 2006

September 15, 2006

I just happened to need a piece of paper so I pulled out this notebook. After I wrote my list for Target shopping. I opened up to the begining & I had totally forgotten that I started this book as a journal back in October 2004 That is almost 2 exact years. And I cannot even believe that was me writting those words. The way i really felt... Is all written down on paper. & when you are writting them, they just flow because you are expressing your feelings & thoughts on paper that comes from w/in your mind and it is telling you how to spell & write. but it's the Soul or Spirit that shines through & comes out in the blue ink. My favorite pens. Well one of.

I'm at such a different place in my life than where I was in October 2004. That was the month that i truely left him by getting the restraining order.. That I later took off. Another moment that i must write about - 2day, is that i saw Him. I saw B. I saw His Escalade and knew his plate number. I was w/ Dave & heading up Rt 1 right near the Sargent St exit. When i passed him, I looked in the driver side window to see if it was really him. Which I think it was. But Dave had his arm up & kinda blocked my view. I wonder if he saw me? I wonder if he ever thinks of me? I wonder if he knows what he did? Does he even realize the pain he put me through? Probally not cuz he says that he was just as hurt. Like I fucked w/ him..

All of a sudden i just got this feeling inside of me.. When i began to write & really FEEL what i was thinking about. i had a good, pleasant, happy or proud... feeling inside.. Cuz i was realizing the anguish & hurt life i was living. It was the beginig [beginning] of my true journey. It was right after the restraining order.. Right after I got my first place. - Alone - It was when i started theraphy [therapy] @ The Victims of Violence unit in Somerville... Then i began to wonder if he saw me? Wonder how He Feels. I suddenly felt disgust, anger & negative. The proud feelings that i had.. Went away & i was looking @ a man that if he did or did not know or if he even ever knows how badly he Fucked with me..

I have FEELINGS!!!!!

This is the second experience I'm having w/ in my body... All of it's connected where as before my mind body & soul were so lost, disconnected or just plain ol shut off, that I now can take notice when I feel. I never knew what it was like to "feel". I missed some important things/happenings in my life due to a upbringing that was emotional but very detached.. To a young 19 year old that was very mature.. instead of detached.. I went NUMB..

Completely NUMB.

I'm extremly happy & proud of where I am at spirtually in my life. Mentally as well. I have come along way. & I have even helped Sarah on the way..

My life - I have watched it go into "full circle" I'm very lucky as well as Blessed 2 be me. These days are precious to me & i have filtered out all negative aspects.. From friends, to thoughts, to actions.. And I am watching myself "right before my very eyes" or shall I say. I am FEELING tremendous changes inside my mind. That now connects w/ my body that speaks to my soul. & when I feel the need to express my true emotions it comes out of the very Blue pen w/ as much love as a mother has for her child. I love myself & I will continue to stay positive & live life How I want 2. By my Rules.. My dignity & pride will remain Strong Baby.. Peace. Love. J 06

June 16, 2015

Therapy

It had been a long two years since I was out from under my trafficker. Though my journey was difficult, freedom tasted good, and I was healing. I had feelings! Can you hear the excitement in my words?! My body, mind and spirit were connecting after years of being shut off. I didn't last long at the Victims of Violence Center, but the therapist gave me some great tools and understanding about my trauma. I know I was self-medicating by abusing Oxycontin, cocaine and alcohol, but something was noticeably happening inside of me.

I was thinking about getting myself sober. My brother passed away of a drug overdose in June 2006, so at the time I wrote this diary entry, I didn't want my mother to lose both her children to drugs. But I was addicted to drugs, money and the fast lifestyle.

I remember the first time another addict told me I had a drug problem. We had been up for a few days. He was smoking crack, and I was snorting lines of cocaine mixed with Oxycontin. While in my kitchen, he looked at me and asked, "Jazz, do you think you have a drug problem?" My response sounded like someone in deep denial. "NO! As long as I have enough money, it's never gonna be a problem".

If you don't know by now, drug addiction is not a moral issue. It is a sickness that has no cure, but thankfully it can be treated. It wouldn't be until January 1, 2007 that I entered into my first detox. Try after try, I finally got it. On September 19, 2007, I put down the heroin and got off the streets. I have never sold my body since then. But, I have relapsed with drugs. Maybe I'll save those stories for another time.

Little girls don't dream about becoming a prostitute or drug addict. Something goes very wrong along the way. Because of the lack of options, she may fall prey to the life, which you know is no life at all.

October 17, 2006

Well i didn't get 2 write last night. i had a tough day. That's 4 sure! The past few days Chris & I have been argumentive. We got into a blow out & he exploded & broke up with me. There is way more to the story but I am actually high at the moment & can barely write... I cannot see the pages.

I'm very tired.. Very Drained.

I will write later...

June 25, 2015

My New Normal

The drugs were taking over. I was using Oxycontin on a daily basis to cope with the pain of being sex trafficked and the loss of my brother. I could not deal with life on life's terms. Using drugs became my normal. Selling my body and drugs, sleeping with drug dealers, drinking Wednesday through Sunday and always having major issues in my life—this all became NORMAL.

When you begin abusing substances, you really believe you have it under control. You do not foresee how your life will eventually unravel. If you are lucky enough to not die in active addiction, then you are walking around dead on the inside. I was on a suicide mission. Nothing really mattered when I was using because I was compelled daily to feed the monster that was living inside of me. It was like an electrical switch that could not be turned off.

I did have moments of clarity, and I entered into another relationship with a good guy, but he struggled with addiction. He always believed in me and wanted to see me live the life he knew I was capable of, but he was just as broken as I was.

In recovery, we say, "Two dead batteries won't start a car." That was us. We saw the good in each other and wanted each other to succeed, but we were too broken and addicted to be of any good to each other. He introduced me to AA and NA meetings because he got into recovery as a teenager. Sadly, this past June was a year since his death. He lost his battle with addiction, and I am still heartbroken about it. My prayers are with his family.

I have seen many lives taken by this disease. I will continue to speak out about substance abuse and talk about the need for better treatment options for active addicts. The other day, I spoke with some service providers who work with victims of trafficking. They mentioned that most of the women they work with are addicted to heroin or cocaine, but there are not enough detox beds in Massachusetts.

So sit with this for a moment: Picture a woman who is being sex trafficked. She has the courage to get out of the game, but she has a drug addiction. She calls around for a detox bed, but there is a two-week waitlist. I'm not sure if you have ever been dope sick, but I am here to tell you that it is brutal. If she is lucky enough to be working with an advocate, she will know that she cannot get into a safe home or domestic violence shelter until she is sober and medically cleared. So, what are her choices at that point?

Until we realize how closely substance abuse and sex trafficking are linked, we will not empower sex trafficking victims to become survivors.

November 10, 2006

Well seems that i have already thought of using this book as a journal. I wrote a lil note on the cover.. & I was just using it to write down the AA meetings i have gone 2 & liked. Yes AA. I can't believe it. I never in my life thought i'd need them.. Nor did i ever think i was an addict.. My life has changed so much.

Mark is the best man. He has his problems but who doesn't? I truely love him. He cares about me. He stepped in & helped me realize my addiction. He believed & believes in me.. He is the first man that has ever accepted me 4 me.

So i will keep this book to record my dreams.. My day 2 day thoughts. & ofcourse my AA & Addiction progress. I want to keep the dates.. It's important 2 me cuz I have gone to meetings but then got high.. This is just the begining 4 me..

So it's a struggle.. It's not easy. But i will keep faith & learn this program. 4 me. 4 life. i want to live.

1st meeting - Charlestown -Friday

2nd - Charlestown - monday

3rd E. Boston 7pm Monday

The next week.. & it is a closed group. They study the 12 steps & i really enjoyed it. I happened 2 go on the night they studied the First Step!! They welcomed me.. I spoke & everything. Then i went to Boston last night & it is the Big Book. I loved hearing the people speak & Mark came with me. After two nights of troubles. He had a breakdown on tuesday & then wed's he went & got high. So yesterday i spent time w/ him & threatned to leave the realtionship if he doesn't get help. He knows he has 2. But he's not making the correct steps.

i went 2 the gym.. Felt great about boxing.. the meeting & i had gotten high on weds. as well but he doesn't know. Cuz i want to stay strong for him right now.

July 7, 2015

The 12 Steps of Alcohol Anonymous

I was coming to terms with myself and realizing that I really was a drug addict. That realization falls in line with the first step in Alcoholics Anonymous. "We admitted we were powerless over alcohol and that our lives had become unmanageable." I know it says alcohol but you can replace it with whatever substance you are abusing, even if it is prescribed by a doctor.

It is my understanding that any chemical you ingest, snort or shoot up to take you out of yourself is substance abuse. You can most definitely use the 12 Steps of AA to face the reality that your life has become unmanageable.

For addicts, the thought that you can't use drugs any more may be very difficult to accept. Like many people with substance abuse issues, I repeated this step numerous times. I knew I couldn't live a healthy and productive life and get high, but I was addicted. I didn't start doing drugs with the knowledge that I would get addicted. It is a slippery slope, heading to hell.

Using drugs was one of the best ways to cope because it had instant effects. I was drowning out the fear, shame, anxiety and hopelessness that I felt. Mix my trauma history with a chaotic childhood, and there was a perfect breeding place for addiction to take over.

This is the reason why I currently go into halfway houses and lead support groups for women with substance abuse issues. It is where many trafficked women end up. Most of the women in the groups have been sexually abused as children, then they have been prostituted, trafficked and in relationships involving domestic violence. The cycle of abuse and addiction goes together hand in hand.

The halfway house employees are usually underpaid, and they are understaffed. How can they empower women with this type of trauma history to end the cycle? That's where I come in. I'm transparent with my story and my struggles to empower women, so they can heal from the shame and become the women they were originally designed to be. Most of the women in these programs are someone's mother. It breaks my heart to hear that someone else is taking care of their children. I see the pain in their eyes when they talk about the difficulties they face in recovery and being a mom.

Realize that when a woman in your community suffers, others suffer. I believe we all have a place in the healing journey for her. Please consider giving a donation to my ministry so I can continue running groups and handing out Bags of Hope to women on the streets and in programs. Let's partner together to let her know that she is worth it.

November 21, 2006

Well I'm off & running I guess you could say... I have continued to get high.. Mark & i have not been able to get it 2 gether. It's just to difficult. He wants 2 rush & i want to take it slow. I still know that I'm not ready.. Proof that I'm still using. So I really just need 2 get my shit right. I need 2 stop this bullshit & get REAL Help. I have to stop using.. It's not getting me anywhere. I will try to get help.

July 21, 2015

Perception

Exiting the commercial sex trade and trying to get it together, is nearly impossible when you have a drug addiction. This cycle continues for many years for the majority sex trafficked or prostituted women and girls. My emotional pain, shame and trauma were intense. With loads of debt, a drug habit and daily life responsibilities, I didn't know how to support myself financially. Prostituting myself was a means of survival.

As I look back, I cannot believe the way I perceived my life. I would lie to myself because I always felt that I was the one in control. I told myself that the men who purchased me were the tricks, and I was smarter for taking their money. This way I could make myself feel powerful, secure and confident in that role. I was trading my body with strangers for drugs and money. In reality, I was being purchased, abused and controlled. Even though I created a sense of control, I lived in fear.

To all the women and girls out there: The sex industry is not a means of women's empowerment. It is oppression. You can share my story with anyone who tells you that the sex industry is a great way to make money and get ahead.

To all the sex buyers: I never enjoyed my time with you. Please seek healing for your sex addiction.

To the traffickers: I pray you realize that you are being lied to by the over-glamorization of money, sex and crime. Yes, I know you will say that sex sells, but selling a body destroys the soul.

This September, it will be eight years since I have been out of the game. While recovery is messy and hard, I wouldn't go back to living the way I did. My current struggles with relationships are real, but I would rather struggle than live a lie. Although I am healed from the shame surrounding what happened to me, I know that I am not my past. But it sure has shaped me into who I am today.

I am broken. But by the grace of God, I am loved.

December 20, 2006

I woke up around 6am & had a weird sense of something.. I realized that I dreamed about my brother.. The dream went like this: I was @ a beach. It looked like Revere Beach. Where we used to sit when I was a kid. The waves were hudge & i was in the water w/ a circle raft. I was telling someone how beautiful the water was.. it was crystal clear. I went under water.. & Then came up. I was then in a small pool of water w/ an edge to sit on. It seemed like my family was there. I was holding a kid. A child. w/ dark hair. The sun was beating down hard. And as i looked up, I saw my brother i front of me w/ his shirt off in a lounge chair. Saying to me - "you got dark or you got color or you got burned" I can't remember which one. And I agreed. Looked down @ the child & he had on a gold necklace. Then I remember sitting down by the water & i was on a lounge chair w/ the kid still in my arms but also there was these big shells.. They had these little clicking things inside of them. I got nervous & put the shells down on the chair. & I got up. As I got up my family was behind me in the water rinsing off, ready to leave. I started to jump around cuz I felt like the little things were on me. - Just like in real life I had little things on me from the water when I was a kid, Carol was there too. So then i woke up.

I went pee and saw Benz and petted him and then I saw a light go by my window and thought it was strange cuz I never see headlights or lights go by. I then remembered the dream and thought of my brother, my drug addiction & feel back asleep. i want to. I really want to stop doing drugs & get my life 2gether. I have to stop this craziness. I am hurting. And I am ruining my credit. Not just financially but w/ my parents & people around me.. This all has to stop.. This new year will be different. I swear. I promise to myself and my brother.

July 23, 2015

The Dream

This entry is significant because I was in active addiction and still writing in my journal when I had some clarity. I'm grateful for this process of looking back because it all has meaning now, eight and a half years later.

Understand that my brother died of a drug overdose earlier that year in June. I was struggling with that loss, but not really grieving because I was abusing drugs. His death was one of the reasons I thought about getting sober.

I loved looking back to this entry because I find it interesting how life works out. In that dream there was a child with dark hair who I held in my arms.

When I got sober for the final time in 2007, I was six months into my recovery, and I got pregnant. Yes, it was a one-time deal. I had gotten sober and found the Lord, so I thought EVERYONE should follow suit. That was not so for the guy I was dating while I was using drugs and working in the life. We got together one night, and I told him all about my new life. He didn't want anything to do with my spirituality or my Step 9, Make Amends, that night. As I reflect, I realize that I wasn't going to see him to apologize for the insanity of our prior relationship, but I was looking for validation and attention, a common theme throughout my life.

Needless to say, God is in the business of working out all things for our good, even when we fail. But I was scared. I had no idea how I was going to work out this pregnancy thing. I was just getting my life on track. How was I going to be a single mom? I knew that I could not abort another baby. So I prayed, sought counsel and wisdom from the people in my church community. They were very supportive and loving.

I also find it cool that I literally went under the water, like in my dream, and was baptized when I was six months pregnant.

The best part of this story is that my son was conceived on my brother's birthday, which happened to be Easter in 2008. Talk about Resurrection Sunday! I named this bundle of joy after my brother, and yes, he has dark hair. Just like the child in the dream.

Becoming a mother has changed my life in tremendous ways. I always joke and say that I never even liked kids before I had them. While that's true, I now see the gifts I have been given, and I wouldn't trade them for the world.

Taking care of children is another reality for women exiting sex trafficking. Many of them have children before, after or during the time of the trafficking. It is imperative that we give them resources and opportunities for healing and recovery, so they can become all they were meant to be. These women are a child's mom and someone's daughter.

Editor's Note:

According to research done by neuroscientist Eric Nesler and his team, addiction permanently changes the brain. Addictive drugs can produce a protein called DeltaFosB. This protein accumulates in the brain cells each time the drug is used. It causes irreversible damage to the dopamine system and makes a person more susceptible to other addictions. DeltaFosB not only helps to trigger addictions, but also it works to maintain addictions. The accumulation of DeltaFosB also occurs with non-drug addictions such as compulsive running. Researchers have called this protein "a sustained molecular *switch* for addiction".

Also, when some addictive drugs of abuse are taken, they can release two to 10 times the amount of dopamine that natural rewards, such as eating and sex, release. These results were found in research done on freely moving rats and reported by G. Di Chiara and A. Imperato in the Proceedings of the National Academy of Sciences of the U.S. in 1988.

Chapter 7

Diary: Year 2007

January 2, 2007 Somerville Hospital - Detox

2007.. I cannot believe that it's another year.. Another year has gone by & I've tried to get better on my own but.. I haven't succeeded... That's why as I write this I am laying on white sheets that drape over, on a very smooshie but small twin size bed.. in a Detox room in Somerville. I'm wearing a super fly pair of blue scrubs.. Baggy pants & a oversize shirt. They said I could keep it. Gee Thanks..

So yes, I admitted myself into Somerville Hospital. I got real tired of not getting anywhere doing the same insane Bullshit day after day!! i can't believe that I got involved in what eventually became a serious habit. These things took over my life.

I am living @ home with my parents. Wich is soo much better 4 me. i used to get up everyday, do a jam or try 2 get one. Sit home. Do nothing or maybe watch Tv. Run a few errands.. Sleep till 2pm. Cuz I was up so late from the night before. I mean i just lived terrible.. I was getting Bad. Nothing mattered 2 me anymore. I barely paid my bills. I only worked 2 survive. I lost all of my responsibilty, respect & self esteem. I was mixing coke & jams.. Sometimes doing the coke alone.. That was never me! Coke was never even my drug of choice! But i started to mix it. Cuz the jams

149

would make me so tired i liked 2 get that rush of coke so i'd do alot, line after line.. Then slow down immeditaly w/ a jam.

I put myself in a few bad situations while i was out there getting high. I hung out w/ some really crazy people. i didn't care.. But now i want 2 change my life sooo much. like i can't believe that i was excited 2 come here. I was calling & calling Danvers Cab & health & there was nothing. Then i said 2 myself Fuck it. Let me call Somerville cuz Katie went there. So i called & Bam. The lady said 2 be there by 5pm! i called my mom right away & felt so happy. i got high 2day. Cuz i knew it would be like the last time. Fuck it. And i only did it cuz I worked & made some money. Otherwise I couldn't have. Plus i wanted to in some sick way.. I wanted 2 really have 2 suffer when i got here. I want to be so sick & so miserable for all the bullshit i have caused. I'm so mad @ myself. Very disapointed & I don't want 2 come back here again. I want 2 get it together & make sense out of life. I don't want 2 chase that drug. That addiction. I want 2 b free of it. Free of it!! I want to be clean & healthy. Clean & happy & sober!!

I pray that i make it. Please Chris be my angel on my shoulder. Please Renee make me, or help me remember how bad my life has become & nonnie Gracie. Please help me become the woman i should be. let me make my mom & dad proud. let me see our family through sober eyes. I want a good life. I want to be @ peace with myself.

I just spoke at the last meeting of the night.. And i was sooo shaky inside.. But boy, did it feel good 2 speak. I'll write again.

In the name of the lord, Jesus & the Divine.

My Divine.

May i get to a place of serenity & let me feel that there is hope 4 me.. Amen. Love Jazz

*Jam = Oxycontin

July 28, 2015

A New Name

I want to stress that the guilt and shame a woman feels can keep her silent or resistant to help and change. Let me explain. Initially, I was attracted to B because of his riches and power. Those things made me feel like I was successful. But soon, B gradually used my vulnerabilities to exploit me. I felt weak and useless, as if I could not do or be anything without him.

At the time, I wasn't aware of this fact. Therefore, I internalized the abuse and blamed myself, which made me feel guilty. I felt ashamed the very first time I exchanged money for my body with a stranger. The memory is still burned in my brain. I blamed myself for getting into the relationship with my trafficker and for staying so long. During the five years, I tried very hard to please him and to earn his love. Learning to trust again has taken great courage.

My mind, body and soul were damaged by the time I exited my trafficking situation. I thought the only way to financially support myself was to return to prostitution. I tried making minimum wage, but it wasn't paying my bills or supporting my drug addiction. I made myself feel better about what I was doing by considering myself a high-priced escort.

As I look back, I see the truth in my words. In all the diary entries, I can clearly remember how I was feeling at that specific time—hopeless and depressed. I wanted to suffer and be punished for all the havoc I thought I caused in my life. However, the reality is that I was a victim of sex trafficking. I just didn't know it. I was carrying guilt and shame that did not belong to me.

Today, I am grateful for recovery. I finally have been freed from prostitution, addiction, shame and guilt. Those things no longer control or define me. I am called by new names—they have been given to me by my Creator. I am called chosen, redeemed, forgiven, beloved and a child of God.

January 18. No, 17th, 2007 @ 11:23pm

Well what a year so far... 3 weeks into a New Year & I've been to Detox, meetings & almost on the verge of a mental breakdown.. Seriously. Detox was an experience.. Maybe I'll write about it some day... But what has my pen going @ the moment. Is that I am @ my lovely house.. My parents house... & My mom has once again proved that she is a control freak. Nevermind. severely depressed and plain miserable. i don't know how my father deals w/ her Bullshit, like why & who the fuck would want 2?? That's the million $ question.

I'm high, so lets get that straight. #2 Mark has been ruining my life more & more. His new thing is telling my parents that I'm an "Escort" & gave them my work phone number & emailed my mom telling her the website & my "name". Then has the audacity to email me (cuz he cannot call) & tell me to go home & check my her email. Cuz he sent it @ like 4 this afternoon. He was pissed cuz i said "alot of hurtful things" Meanwhile he has been telling me what a jerk i am.. & How he wants to kill himself. The last straw was "I'm goin to the Hotel & taken the 30 Valium & leaving a note & blaming it all on you". I couldn't take it anymore, so i called his sister.. & then Sean also got on the phone.. Well that was it. He had enough & went & acted a fool.

I'm soo tired of his drama. I'm beating myself up because i cannot understand what the fuck i was thinking. Deb says that i wasn't aware & my judge of character were way out of whack.. & i know this because i was active in my addiction.

I'm highly disappointed in myself. The drug abuse, the lies, the hurt, the pain, the denial, the lack of self esteem, Respect, & honor.. I have lost it all inside of Jasmine.. I am empty. The only thing left is my small lack of self control. Otherwise i would not be here at my parents. Writting in my Journal., As I almost go into a Nod... My eyes cross..

Jees, I feel better after writting just that little. I feel like i have soo much more to share.

Peace.

May my Higher Power Help me.. in life & love.

August 4, 2015

Miracles

That entry is funny and sad all at the same time. It is also pretty amazing that I thought, one day I might write about my time in detox. And here I am, eight years later, really writing about it. I would have never imagined my life the way it is now—sober, alive and on a journey of healing. I am facing my past in such a transparent and vulnerable way that some days I want to delete these reflections and just move on. But I simply cannot do that. I have been given too much to turn around now.

I am speaking for those who can't find their voices. I am allowing this process to show the world that recovery is hard, but worth it. People who may never witness what God can do in someone's life can read about it here. I want you to know that healing from trauma is possible, and God is still in the business of performing miracles. I am proof and so are many survivors across the globe.

I must say that some parts of the dairy entry are embarrassing. Today, I would never speak to my mother or think about her in that way. I now see her through eyes of compassion, love and understanding. My parents were not perfect. They have their own struggles. But I will say, no matter what, they were always physically available for me. I am sure that having both parents living together in the same home created a sense of stability for me. They have lived in the same house for 20+ years. I had a place to return to. It was a place that I called home, even when I hated it. They accepted me and supported me the best way they knew how. They still do, and for that I am grateful.

I have witnessed the devastating effects in the lives of young girls and boys when their home isn't a safe place. Now, I can see that having a place to return to saved me from more years out on the streets.

I see how people end up in even worse situations with no one to watch over them. I see that they are even more vulnerable when their homes are filled with sexual abuse, addiction and violence. Therefore, it is vital that we create safe, stable and nurturing homes for our own families and to support women as they recover from sex trafficking, prostitution and substance abuse. Everyone needs a place to call home.

I am also realizing how my choices in intimate relationships were so damaging to my soul. I repeatedly chose the biggest lunatic in the place. After my trafficker, I seemed to gravitate toward the guy that had a criminal record the size of an encyclopedia. Why is that? I still haven't figured out all that.

Sadly, both those men I mention in my diary, Mark and Sean, have died in the past two years. Mark was a sweet guy, but he was on a suicide mission from the day I met him. He abused some hard-core drugs and said he would never do heroin because that's how his father died. Unfortunately, he ended up addicted to the needle and overdosed. My heart is still saddened by his death.

However, Sean was far from sweet. He was quite scary actually. He was the first person to shoot me up with heroin. We met in detox after he was released from the hospital. He came up to the detox unit bruised and bloody from his last run. He ran the streets hard and was known to terrorize people who interfered with his intense drug habit. We didn't hang out long because at that time, I was in and out of detoxes. Soon enough, I would move on to find another guy to run the streets with.

I was a lost and running on empty. I was masking the pain of the past with relationships and drugs. It got me absolutely nowhere. Have you been there, too?

I was seeking more, but I was spiritually blind. Today, I have found my hope and deepest desires met in Jesus. I have been made complete in Him. Not perfected, but made complete and whole. I find comfort knowing that the Creator of the universe delights in me and loves me unconditionally. I find peace in His word. I was like the Samaritan woman at the well who had a life-changing encounter with the Son of God. Just like her, I was thirsty for more. I have found living water in my growing relationship with Christ. I was living in sin, far away from

having a connection to God and others. I just didn't know it until I accepted Jesus into my heart as my Lord and Savior.

How about you? Have you found what you've been searching for?

January 26, 2007

Just 4 today i will do my best. I will keep my thoughts positive & calm.

Just 4 today I will live a sober life & not dwell on all the sadness I endure.

Just 4 today I will smile & be nice to people & share my story if they wish to hear.

I'm sitting in my second detox in one month. I came in yesterday after I came out & used right away. I then continued to use & finally shot heroin w/ Sean. But luckily by the Grace of God I had tooken a suboxone in the morning, well afternoon. So when he shot me up i didn't really get high. The next day i got Oxy's & went to Danielle's house. & I called every detox In Mass that would take freecare. I got a bed here in plymouth @ highpoint. I'm very grateful to have made it here & that i didn't hurt myself.

I could have OD because of the suboxne, plus Sean shot me up once, then he shot up himself, had this crazy reaction. He was scary actually freakin me out. So he then shot me up again.. couldn't find the vein. Then again 3rd time. My arm is bruised & had a lump. We spent the next few hours together & he was yelling like he had turetts syndrome. Acting like a total nut case.

I couldn't believe that we went to a total crackhouse, bought dope, went to CVS, bought needles. We shot up in his mothers bathroom. Where from his last run, had blood squirts all over the ceiling. He is totally unstable & i now know & realize that i have to take care of myself & not allow anyone to violate me in anyway. I feel very used. I paid for the dope, the jams, bought him clothes, paid for dinner, movies & suboxne. That he abused.. & then I pulled money out of my account making it a negative balance. He is definitly in a bad spot right now. But i cannot do anything 4 him. I must do what i gotta do 4 myself.. He leaned on me way to much.

I'm so happy to be in here & that I'm getting another chance to do this right. My recovery needs time to progress.

August 18, 2015

Finding Our Voices

That entry explains how the disease of addiction progresses and takes an addict to places they never imagined.

Today, I had the opportunity to share this exact journal entry with young girls who live in a group home. These girls are between the ages of 13 and 17. They are all living there because something traumatic has happened to them. Some of the girls have stable parents and homes. But many do not. I can bet that most of the girls I spoke with today are in foster care or in the Massachusetts system for the Department of Children and Families. They do not have a safe, stable and nurturing home to return to. This saddens me, and it makes me angry. Some of their mothers may share a story similar to mine, and that's why their daughters are not living with them. If no one intervenes, the cycle continues.

That's why I care enough to step into the gap and share my story. I believe that prevention work can only begin when we are vulnerable, transparent and honest with our OWN stories. Stories that are—raw, powerful and beautiful.

I shared my story of survival, faith and victory alongside another survivor today. While our stories were different, they were also very similar. Her trafficker was a neighborhood friend whose father was a trafficker and mother was a sex trafficking victim. My trafficker was a drug dealer, whose hustle progressed into pimping/trafficking.

Both of our drug addictions started as a way to numb the pain from our experiences. The drugs became our pimps.

This is what happens to many American girls and women who are sex trafficked. Many will become the junkies on the street corner that will steal your wallet if we have the chance. If you have seen us, you may have judged us as a hooker or dirty prostitute. Maybe you think that we wanted to be there. But I am here to tell you the truth. What you are not seeing is the underlying string of unfortunate events that put us there.

Little girls have good dreams for their future; they don't want to be prostitutes. I wanted to be a veterinarian or teacher. I managed to get my cosmetology license when I was 18 years old.

Let me reassure you that we do recover, and when we do, we find OUR VOICE. When that voice is united with many other survivor voices, we create change. We bring healing into the darkest of places because we aren't afraid to walk through those places this time. We have already been there. We are Overcomers.

Just for today: I want to live and enjoy life. To do that, I will put my recovery first.

January 27, 2007

So I'll pick up where I left off. Yesterday was an OK day. I got to talk to a counselor & tell her my "shit". Which felt good & some tears ran down my cheeks. I also got to speak @ a meeting. - a girls group met & my lovely roomates volunteered me to speak cuz the topic was Domestic abuse & we had just been talking about it in our room. The roomates think I'm "strong & smart" & Maybe cuz I'm a little older they look up to me a little. So I spoke about my experience w/ B & explained how the mental abuse really got me messed up. & I came out of "the fog" & hung out w/ the wrong people & started using. We go inturupted but the girls asked if i could finish my story.. Which i did. & it felt awesome to talk & share.. It seemed like alot of the women have gone through the same "Domestic Abuse" Realtionships. So it felt great to get that off my chest. like they say, you are only as sick as your secrets.

I'm feeling optomistic about my Recovery & the Steps i have to take. I have to follow the "suggestions" & stick to them & make sure I never become Complacient w/ where I am in my journey.. I'm going to take all the education & knowledge & use it as my tools. I will begin to not just say things but i will do things, like go to meetings.. get a sponser. And most of all, I promise to myself that I will Respect, Cherish, Worship & be honest @ all times.. And remember to love myself & not allow anyone to step over my personal boundaries.. I always manage to actract the type of men that want to latch on.. & I just get super emotional & attach myself but only 4 a little while.. I get bored & break their heart. Or i allow themto treat me a certain way.. even if I don't like it. And I'm getting better @ Realizing "Red flags".. But as I grow in my Recovery & Life. I will begin to get better with myself & expect to get treated with respect & dignity cuz I will have more self "esteem" & when I can finally give up work.. Or come to an honest acception w. it.

I know my life is never going to be happy. I'm never going to be at peace w/ myself. All the lies to my family & close friends. And never mind relationships.. I can't seem to get past my own insecurities. Work definitly hinders my growth. I'm thinking that my life hasen't had any value in a long time. And the drugs just covered up all of my pain., fear, loneliness. sadness & made work easy as pie @ times. I know that I'm comfortable w/ numbness & no emotion. Cuz it's all i've known 4 many years.

It's my loyalty & giving ways that get me into trouble. I've never really had any self esteem. if I look back to when is I was 12 Having sex w/ older boys, doing drugs, & then High School w/ Jacob, binge Drinking.. & not having a stable sense of self.. I got into "the game" w/ B & still somewhere in my deep deep thoughts I believe that I'm nothing more than a working girl. & No one will ever love me 4 me.. Cuz that's who I am & what i do.. even if i give it up & keep out of a relationship, I'm afraid of being rejected , used & lied to.

I don't Remember one time where a man told me that i was beautiful or smart or anything positive & felt like he actually meant it. Tricks to regular guys.. They all say it. But it's me that thinks they are just saying it to "fuck me" or "get what they want". I really have to work on my self esteem & get to know who the Hell I am ?! Remember to take one day @ a time. Keep the pace @ a momentum i can handle. Repeat the Serenity prayer. "God please Grant me the Serenity to accept the things I cannot Change, The courage to Change the things I can & the Wisdom to know the Difference."

I want to get a sponser, a substance abuse counselor, & maybe a grief consuler.. But what about the " Post Dramatic[Traumatic] Stress Disorder"? If The drug abuse happend mostly cuz of what i went through w/ B. & now i still work cuz that's what i know & have come to a "very safe place". Well that's what I think. Cuz I've been doing it 4 SO long.. The drugs just made it that much easier. I still haven't grieved 4 Rocky, never mind my brother. Drugs have not just taken away my pain & filled my emptyness But they have Doug [dug] me into a Deeper hole of Sadness all my issues have been mostly surpressed & ignored.

I have allowed, Or my addiction has taken away my Spirtuality, my sense of self & self worth. I need to just make it through 2day.. There instead of writting "all the things" I want or have to do.. I took a step back & remembered I can only control one day. Tommorrow will come & when it does I will handle it & do the best i can.. Even if it gets hard. I can always break it down to one minute or one hour. Just Remember to put myself first. My Recovery & Sobrietyare the Most Important factors 2day.. - Jazz. Peace & love - 2007-

August 27, 2015

Nonnie Gracie's Ring

That entry has a lot of expression. It is filled with many questions and reflections. I was a lost young woman who was feeling unloved and unwanted, detoxing from Oxycontin in a rehab center. My past had a hold on me. My future looked bleak as I pondered what life would be like if I gave up prostitution, which I was referring to as work. Now, I know that prostitution should never be called work. That is what my trafficker called it. He told me I would always be nothing more than a dirty prostitute. I knew that there must be more to life, but drugs and prostitution is what gave me my identity.

I found false security, love and power in a life that was filled with lies and torment. I was burying the pain with pills and cocaine. While in detox, I was searching for meaning and trying to find hope. But the grip of addiction wasn't ready to let go. The Serenity Prayer wasn't enough. Self-help and relapse prevention groups were only useful if you *used* the ideas they gave you. I saw the world in black and white. There was no color, no joy, no peace, no love—just emptiness.

My 35th birthday was last week. I was blessed to celebrate it with my small, immediate family. After making a wish and blowing out the candles, my grandmother, who is in her 80's, surprised me with a family heirloom. It was a beautiful diamond ring that was my great grandmother's. Her name was Grace, and I am grateful that my parents gave me that middle name. She passed away when I was about 12 years old. The above entry shows the time that life got difficult for me. When she died, my mother felt that I was too young to attend the funeral and services, so I stayed with my father's parents, who happened to live across the street from my Nonnie Gracie. I can remember standing at the door watching everyone gather at her house, and I wished I could be there. I will always remember her as a funny, outgoing woman and a great cook. Her house was always filled with people, laughter and lots of other craziness. She often swore in Italian. She had a pet cockatiel bird that she named Casey, and he even said bad words!

This ring represents more than a family heirloom. To me, it is a reminder of who I am and who created me. It shows how far I have come in my recovery, how I am loved and cherished by God, how my Father in heaven saw me when I was that little girl grieving the loss of a family member, how He saw me when I was a lost young woman in a detox. He knew my name then and now. He sees me all the time. He cares for me and blesses me beyond my wildest dreams. There is no doubt that God placed this ring on my finger to remind me of His grace—His unchanging and never-ending faithful love and mercy.

Friends, He wants to show you the same kind of forgiveness. Hebrews 4:16 states, "So let us step boldly to the throne of grace, where we can find mercy and grace to help when we need it most." Grace is unmerited favor. We do nothing to deserve it. You don't need to clean up first.

Just call out to Jesus. He is kind and compassionate, ready to fill your aching heart with the peace that you seek.

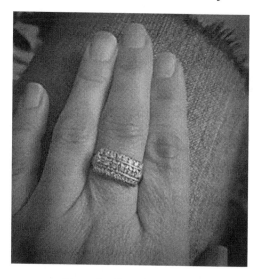

Nonnie Gracie's ring.

February 4, 2007

Ok. another Day in Highpoint Brockton.. I'm having thought of not going to a halfway house. Cuz i know that i can go 2 my moms, meetings.. & work the program.. But truthfully.. I have had thoughts of using... "one more time" just once more. I keep thinking of my dealer & i just want to call Him. But I'm afraid of it. I don't want to waste my life. I want to live & be loved.. & give back. I want to Stay positive.. Please GOD. Help me to get a good life!!

September 24, 2015

Celebrating

I was fighting for my life and trying to keep the urges of using at bay "just one more time". If you've never been addicted to a controlling substance, then you will never understand the difficulty and complexity of recovery. So please don't judge an addict. You have no idea about the battle they're fighting.

There I was in a program, crying out to a God I did not know. I needed someone to save me from myself. I had no idea that it would end up getting worse for me. I would end up relapsing soon after leaving that program. I didn't know how hard getting sober would be! In my situation, it got worse before it got better.

But I am thrilled to tell you, that on Saturday, September 19, 2015, I celebrated eight years of recovery! To me, that means I have never exchanged my body for a place to stay, food, money or drugs. No man has ever purchased me since then.

Rather, I have been ransomed and redeemed by God himself. Isaiah 52:3 states, "For this is what the LORD says: "You were sold for nothing, and without money you will be redeemed." Now, I know that He paid my ransom with His shed blood. It cost His life. But I was willing to surrender my life to Him in order to find freedom. I can see how He is using my pain for His purpose. And for that, I am grateful.

Don't get me wrong, recovery has been extremely difficult at times. I have relapsed on drugs, made plenty of mistakes and wanted to give up. But joy always comes in the morning. My journey has included many gifts—two amazing children, a lot of healing, many supportive and safe friends, lots of laughs, and a loving relationship.

From this beautiful mess, I have learned many lessons. My story and journey matter. There is power when I share in a transparent and authentic way. I've seen many lives changed as a result. I know that if I accept the pain rather than run away from it, I become stronger and wiser. I have learned to face the truth and have peace and rest without using drugs.

Today, I am secure and confident because I am loved by God. Best of all, I have a chance to share that love and give back to many women in need. That is how Bags of Hope Ministries was founded. The ministry is community driven because I believe that it takes the whole community to support and empower women along their journey. We started in 2014, and in two years we have given women more than 800 bags.

February 6, 2007. 8:36pm (Brockton)

Well A few Days ago, I Realized that this journal Does not go in oRder, & it made me think that it's Kinda Like my Life Right now. Crazy, out of order.. & needs to be Re-organized.. So here I am Sitting in Brockton SOAP.. & I met a kid Louie from Worcester.. Street Kid. Shoots Dope & has been through the Ringer.. Tattoo's - Yeah Quite A few.. I like him.. But I got news that I'm outta here 2-morrow - off to a holding.. When i wasn't even Sure if I wanted to go..

But again my higher Power is Directing me when I cannot cuz this is what i need wheater i want to OR Not.. That's a Different StoRY.. I'm sad, scared, afraid of the UnKnown.. & will miss everyone that I met here.. It was a Powerful Group.. Dave from New Bedford, always calls me sweetie & tells me what a good girl I am.. Plus all the haircuts I did. Johnny, the Boxer.. he's a leo and cuts hair too. Gregg, courage & class.. Makes me laugh.. Sherry! too! I came here w/ her from Plymouth & she makes me laugh.. Plus the staff.. I'm Grateful to have met Gordan @ Plymouth. I will Never 4get him.. Jack - here in Brockton - Knowing the light skinned dude, Jason from Chelsea. My world is full of great people & places. I just have to get my place in it secured.. So i don't Slip.. & miss what it has to offer me.. Please Grant me, Strength, Courage & Serenity.. Love me

October 6, 2015

Feeling Safe

I was trying to make the best of the program that I was in. This was definitely a positive step in my early recovery journey. I felt comfortable and safe in that program. And I learned a lot about myself and addiction. Unlike many women, I didn't have a ton of outside pressures, such as drug court, pending criminal charges, children, an abusive partner, debt and so on. Don't get me wrong. My life was insane and chaotic, but still manageable at that time.

I lead eight-week "Safe Haven" groups in a halfway house, and my heart gets heavy when I hear the situations that women face on the outside. I see how these "external pressures" make it more difficult for women to enter and stay in substance-abuse treatment. One of the most difficult topics is children. If you don't have kids, the only way that I can explain the love a parent feels for a daughter or son is that it is like having a piece of your heart walk around outside of your body.

When someone is in active addiction, most times they are in complete denial about how bad the habit is. Situations arise and difficult things happen. Life just seems to spiral out of control because the addiction has taken over. Getting the next fix is the most important thing. It overrides everything. If these circumstances lead to having the child care system take away your kids, it feels like a slow death or a wakeup call to some women.

I haven't met one mother who was happy about her drug addiction, her unstable past and how her situation has put her child at risk. She is not thrilled that she is in a program, but she wants to be the mom her kids deserve. She wants to be the mom she never had. She wants to bake cookies, do homework and play on the floor with her children.

That is where I come in. I teach new skills, offer hope, encourage and empower her to become all that she was designed to be. I let her know that her past does not define her, and she is more than a conqueror! She is worthy and

treasured. So when you have a chance, please offer love and support with boundaries, but don't judge an addict.

February 5, 2007. 3:45pm

So I'm in the wrong mood 2day. #1. When you do something & there is no Reprocusion -- you think nothing of it.. Most of the time. But this is the scenario Louie & I had fooled around yesterday.. & the day before. The first time we were in my room 4 a few mins & we kissed & BlaBla.. Well all day yesterday I could tell that he was really liking me.. He would kiss me in front of people.. & I actually got a little "scared" or uninterested. I think I like to c what i can do.. or who's attention i can get & then when i do.. They fall in love & i move on. Or get bored. I know this isn't good..

But so I then proceeded to flirt & kiss him back. Cuz yes I like "instant" gratifaction.. & fill my 'drug void" w/ good feelings from him.. Which he is aware of as well. So we then Did what we did.. It was fun, exciting. & we are not supposed to be. So it was what it was.. But i soon felt a little.. Umm Cheap.. I mean i did what i did in a Detox Bed.. almost 4getting where i was.. & not caring.. nothing mattered.. It was stupid & i felt Kinda Bad.. But he still said he didn't think any different.. & I know i don't about him.. But it's myself..

So i woke up 2day & got the shit.. Staff & everybody "assumes" Something. I have to learn Self Respect & I know that Being in a place like this.. Comming off Drugs & feeling all the "Bad feelings" isn't where I'll find any Respect. I need to Do it 4 myself.. By myself w/ the help of outside counsolors & a therepist. I need to know that guys are gonna Be attracted to me & that i don't have to give it up.. Just because.. I have it a Little messed up Right now. i know i do. But hopefully i get it under control so i can live a healthy Life..

October 28, 2015

Made New

We all know that old patterns of behavior are hard to break—especially when you have been doing something for a very long time. Giving myself away sexually for free or for money was something I was very used to doing. That is sad.

What saddens me even more is that from a young age, I believed boys only wanted sex. I saw it on TV, in magazines and in my own life. This false belief was reinforced and became a reality because boys either forcefully took it from me, manipulated me into it or they paid me for it. Sometimes I just gave it to them because I wanted them to like me. I based my worth upon my body and how attractive I was to the opposite sex. I was very good at dressing up the outside, but on the inside I was empty, desperate and lonely.

I know that I am not alone in this struggle. This may resonate with many young girls and women today. I wish I had an inspirational story to tell you about how I overcame this in my own life. But to be vulnerable with you for a moment, this is an area in which I still struggle.

In my head, I believe what the Bible says in 2 Corinthians 5:17, "Therefore, if anyone is in Christ, the new creation has come: The old has gone, the new is here!" I have been taught that verse since I came to know the Lord, and I must remind myself that I am not my past. I am loved by God. He sees me as holy, pure and washed clean. I am loveable.

The problem is that it is a slow process to my heart! To understand these words is one thing, but to believe them and heal is another thing. I know that I will press on and continue to seek the Lord and His goodness for restoration. Will you?

February 7, 2007 4:20pm (New Hope - South Weymouth)

Ok.. So i moved again.. I'm now @ a holding.. New Hope in South

Weymouth.. & I was petrafied to leave Brockton.. I made friends there & felt comfortable.. & I know I'm gonna miss my boy :) Plus the staff there was great.. But i got here & the food is wayyyy better! Thank God!! My parents are supporting me.. & I'm feeling the place out.. Girls are on one side.. Absoulutly no contact w/ Boys.. Thank God. it's fun to flirt..but I really need time to myself. I want to get better. & everyday the urges or thoughts to use aren't as bad as the Day before.. Thank God. Cuz i really want to get better & never have to revisit this place or anything like it..

I want to Remember to be Grateful. *Do the next Right thing.. & Ask 4 help when i need it.

I have found a higher Power.. & believe it's working 4 me.. Cuz I'm ready to accept!!

November 5, 2015

Sober Life

I remember having sincere feelings of wanting to get better. Deep down, I desired to live a life that wasn't consumed with getting high. I am pretty sure that most addicts, at some point in their addiction, have those same feelings and thoughts, even when their behaviors say the exact opposite.

For me, putting down drugs and living a sober life has to be one of the hardest things I have ever done. Now, I understand the research that explains why this is so hard, but I didn't understand it when I was trying to get clean.

Let me try to explain. While using drugs, the addict's brain actually creates new neurological pathways and becomes addicted to the mood-altering substance. When detoxing, the brain works against the detox process because the brain is looking for the chemicals it needs to function. Serotonin and dopamine are inhibitory and excitatory neurotransmitters. These natural chemicals help communicate information throughout the body, but they are depleted while the person is using drugs. The constant flood of imitation chemicals from the drugs puts the natural chemicals out of balance.

So when drugs aren't used, the brain thinks, "WHOA HOLD ON! What the F*#$% is going on up in here!" Hence, the person is moody, irritable, irrational and illogical. This is not fun for anyone.

Once I got past that initial stage, thank God, my brain stopped craving the drug so much. However, I still had old behaviors that would end up sending me back out to the streets and relapse.

But that's OK, because I got through it. I was in the beginning stages of recovery, and I was willing to change. I knew that I needed a Higher Power to save me from myself. I just didn't know when or where He would show up.

February 9, 2007 10:07am NewHope

It's my second day here & it's not bad.. I might be here 4 a month.. not bad news.. but I'm still having a hard time accepting that I have to do this & cannot get "high" anymore. It's like a Break-up almost.. One that I'm actually sad about.. I haven't felt "loss" in a long time.. But i gotta stay strong & get the help i need so i never have to do this again.. I got my life that I'm fighting 4.. I'm in control of my destiny & want happiness in my Life.. The halfway house i'm probably going to is womens place in Cambridge. Which is cool. It's close to home. I always wanted to live in the city. & will be able to get to meetings & see my family. Which i miss so much. But i feel Ok today.. The urges are not as strong.. urges or thoughts. I just got 2 keep reminding myself Oxi's* are no longer apart of my life.. God keep me strong & safe.. peace & love.

*Oxi's = Oxycontin

December 3, 2015

Early Recovery

I remember every substance abuse counselor I ever met would always suggest to me that I needed further treatment. And I remember always wanting to punch them in the face. It didn't sound inviting to live in a halfway house with 15 other women who were coming off drugs and being told what to do by the staff. It seemed scary!

I didn't want to become addicted to Oxycontin. But after I became addicted to it and thought I was living a glamorous life, the idea of giving it all up was horrifying. It truly does feel like a loss or a death because my main coping skill was gone! I had to take off the mask. There I was: a hot mess.

Learning to stay sober and live one day at a time was something that would end up saving my life. But it wasn't what I wanted to do! Getting sober and staying sober takes tremendous effort within the inner self. Early recovery is hard. Most of the time, I hated myself and my life. The constant urge to use, the nightmares, the recurring thoughts about what I went through, the triggers, the impulses that always got me into trouble, the shame, the guilt—all of that and more happens when we come off drugs.

But that stuff didn't kill me like I thought it would. It only made me stronger, wiser and grateful. If you are in early recovery or thinking about getting sober, I want you to know

that you are worth it. Keep fighting the good fight. I am living proof that life gets better, but it takes time.

February 11, 2007

Well another day here in paradise @ new hope. My mom & non are comming up to visit me. Bella was gonna come 2 but the staff said no - only outside & it's to cold.. So that put a bummer on things. Plus the kid from C-town that was passin me notes got in some kind of trouble yesterday so he won't even look @me.. So that "good feeling" went away which i know is all For the Better it just leaves me here by myself w/ my Raw emontions [emotions] 2 deal with like everyone else that's gonna succeed w/ Recovery..

just cuz i got a pretty face & ass w/ purchased Tits Doesn't make me any better & i have to stop that shit. Cuz i think i'm used to getting a guy easily.. & first it's a challenge i pick em - feel em out & then when i get em.. I play 4 a while to fill my needs.. & move on.. That's not Really nice..

So I'll shut up & put up w/ myself, sober & in my own skin 4 once.. I just need a little help from GOD.. Please keep me strong & safe. Jazz xoxo

December 10, 2015

Fighting the Good Fight

There I was—naked, ashamed and angry.

Not filling the void with destructive things and learning to have peace and rest are some of the greatest challenges in early recovery. I hated myself because I was filled with trauma, fear, shame and guilt. I had no drugs to make the feelings go away!

I had become the aggressor and toyed with the minds of boys and men after my trafficking experience. After all, men paid me to have sex with them. I had to smile, manipulate and lie to make them believe that I was enjoying myself. Since that experience, I have struggled to maintain healthy lasting relationships with men.

I felt different being in treatment because I had done some horrible things that put me deep into drug addiction in the first place. What I didn't know was that most of the women in the treatment center had probably experienced some of the same horrific circumstances. But no one was talking about it.

Because I experienced sexual violence at the young age of 13, thoughts about my body image and sexuality were not healthy. Most often, boys found me attractive and easy. I wanted them to like me and accept me, so I gave them whatever they wanted sexually. I wasn't happy doing that and was reluctant most of the time, but the need to be loved was stronger than my understanding of it all. On two occasions when I refused sex, it was taken from me. Most of the details are blurry because of blackouts caused by excessive drinking and drugging. I was drinking and popping pills around 12 or 13 years old. I was depressed, struggling in school and considered a slut, whore and ho. You name it. I was called it.

Fast forward a few years, and then my body was for sale. At 19 years old, I ended up being paid for exactly what was taken from me when I was a young girl. Day after day for eight years, my body was used and abused. I remember the manipulating words my trafficker used during the grooming process to get me to believe that becoming his bottom bitch would be a good idea. He said, "You're already having sex, so why don't you just get paid for it." I now know that using my body for monetary gain gave me a sense of security because I felt in control. The reality was, and still is, that it's a false security. I was out of control. I had a pimp controlling my mind and body for his financial gain. If it wasn't the pimp, the drugs were controlling me.

My heart breaks for the lost, little girl I was, and for every other girl who has experienced sexual violence. Something that is supposed to be sacred and precious should not be taken or sold. For those of you who have been victimized, I want to tell you that it was not your fault. You didn't ask for it because of the way you were dressed or because of the way you acted. I know self-blame is the most natural response.

Healing does come. I'm not going to lie and say that it's easy. It does take a lot of inside work to feel whole and worthy again. I know this because some days I still struggle. What I will say is that it is worth the good fight. You are worthy of more.

February 12, 2007 10:05am - At NewHope

Ok, still here & it's getting easier. Each new day is a blessing.. The struggle is over.. I don't have to get "high" or get off E* just to start my day.. The girls here are comming around & one got kicked out 4 being w/ a guy.. I'm guilty cuz me & A Dude passed a few notes.. & Then on Sat i think he may have gotten in trouble cuz we haven't Really even looked @ each other. Which was a little sad cuz i was getting my "void filled" & then it was taken away.. I don't like that. But that's Life. & I'm not that needy that it will run me outta here.

Yesterday was good cuz my Mom & Non came 2 visit me. My Mom is still having a hard time w/ "the Disease" & Addiction, cuz it was Oxi's & she thinks if i never tried it I would have never gotten in this place! i try to tell her about the progression.. but it's hard. So i just love & pray 4 her..

Plus last nite Jack from Brockton SOAP came in to do a commitment & we talked. i was happy to hear that Louie was still there & Gregg was getting placed. Johnny i guess left to go c his mom. I hope he stays safe. All i can do i pray 4 them. & it made me realize that Someone prayed 4 me to get where I am. So GOD Does work through people. no matter How Big or small the Situation.. you just have to be open & allow him in. I just want to be better & be a good person.

GOD Grant me the Serenity to accept the things i cannot change. The Courage to Change the things i can & the wisdom to know the difference. Peace & Love Jazz

*Get off E = street term meaning when an addicted person wakes up they need to get high in order to function throughout the day.

December 15, 2015

Prayers

If you are reading this and trying to get out of a situation and get clean and sober, or if you are praying for someone to get out of a situation and get clean and sober, I have two words for you: prayer matters.

No matter how big or small the problem, God hears and God sees. I am living proof.

This entire process of looking back and moving forward has blown me away. Not only has it helped me see my story more clearly, but also it helps other women who are struggling. It has shown me that God always has been interested in reaching me, loving me and redeeming all I have experienced. He empowers me to share my story with the world. Through this, people can experience the living hope and glory of Jesus, our true Savior.

Just last week on December 6, we celebrated my mom's birthday at my grandmother's house. This grandmother was the same Nonnie who came to visit me while I was in treatment. After we sang Happy Birthday, she pulled out an old sticky note that she found while cleaning a few days earlier. I don't know the exact date of it, but I will show the picture below so you can read it for yourself. You will be amazed at how God really does work in our lives, even when we have no idea that it is happening.

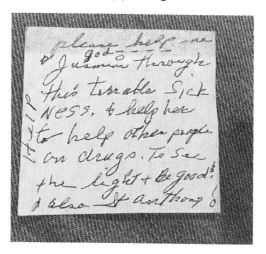

Nonnie Lil's post-it note prayer.

February 14, 2007 Valentines Day - NewHope

Well it's another Day here in Paradise New Hope. 4 girls left due to using drugs & they were the one's who gave me a problem. So it was obvious they weren't ready 4 Recovery. I got a letter from Louie 2day. He's still in Brockton & has an interview 2day.

On the other hand i talked to my little Secret Note passin guy Jimmy. He's polish? & Irish? (lol) & we decied to send each other letters.. instead of pass em. Which makes sense.. Yeah Right. As long as I keep my Recovery upfront, i have Nothing to worry about. I'm goin to women's place 4 Sure. So i can't wait to get that on the move. Other than that I'm feeling good. No obession about drugs 2day. & I'm getting used to being here. getting better @ Dealing w/ the fact that this is where I have to be..

Stay Strong.. Peace Love

December 17, 2015

My Beautiful Mess

Reflecting on my journey, I can understand just how fast time goes by. Now that I have eight years of recovery time under my belt, I am learning that life really is a gift. I do not take it for granted. I have witnessed difficult circumstances and situations that change life in the blink of an eye. "This too shall pass," was a saying that I learned in early recovery, and it drove me nuts! I was very impulsive and could not delay gratification for the life of me. Even waiting for a bus was difficult.

My recovery has been very difficult, but beautiful at the same time. I like to call it "my beautiful mess" because my mistakes and mishaps have made me stronger and wiser. I have definitely learned from them. I have noticed that when I have an attitude of gratitude, it helps me stay positive and experience peace. When I am grateful for the simple things in life, such as being clean and sober and having a safe place to rest my head at night, I realize that God is good and trustworthy. He has provided many blessings and provisions

for me that took me to where I am today. My faith has grown, and I have experienced what I was looking for my entire life— unconditional love and acceptance.

February 27, 2007

Hi. Well i haven't gotten 2 write.. Since I've been ON a Little Vacation from new Hope.. I have to change this pen.. WOW Much better. So anyways i even feel weird writting.. Like i can't. I'm in Charlestown in a Motel w/ the kidd (Jim) i was passin notes 2 @ new hope in S. Weymouth. We got kicked out last sunday. So it's been 9 days & we've been stayin @ Zoe's & this Motel. A experience I'll never 4get. ONE that i'm Determined 2 not Re-Live.

Me & Jim have gotten Real Close & i even Got my 30 Day Chip @AA. i've experienced a Shit load of Life these past Days.. Clean & Sober. I've gone to extreme lengths for my Sobirety.. Due to the fact that my addict & impulsive behavior got me Kicked out of a Really good program & now i'm shelter bound. Waiting to get into my Half-Way House.. I could have just given up & gone back home but i want to finish out what i started & learn a lesson from every mistake - or decison.

I've seen my higher Power work through others & come through for Me. i pray to stay strong, for the courage & wisdom i need to get through this. My desire to use is way less than the Desperation i have to stay clean. I have to Stay Clean.. I have so much motivation & want a happy - Good & fullfiling Life. I'm willing to go to any lengths.. Which i sure have.. This week 4 SURE. Keep me focused. Keep me strong. Peace Love- Jazz

December 22, 2015

Accomplishments

I remember those days like they were yesterday. Getting my 30-day chip at an AA meeting was a big accomplishment! Seeing other alcoholics and drug addicts living productive,

good lives was encouraging in those early days. I was out on the street with no stable place to rest my head, and I wasn't getting high. Not yet.

It was rough. We were beating feet all over Cambridge, Boston and Lynn. It was a typical winter in New England—freezing cold with late buses and trains and snowy, mushy sidewalks. My feet were always frozen. Let's just say that it was not a good time to get kicked out of a program! I cherished the warm pair of socks my friend Zoe gave me. (I still have them, even though there is a hole in the toe). I also loved the drop-in center in Somerville. Often, we would go there to just sit and warm up for a little bit. A sweet older woman worked at the motel where we stayed. She knew Jimmy and his family. She would help us out with rides and give us food from time to time. My family was also supportive and helped me when I needed it.

Loving and supporting an addict in early recovery isn't easy. We are an emotional mess and all over the place. One minute, we are motivated and pumped up to be sober; the next minute, we want to forget it all and get high.

The desire to use would come back. I would end up relapsing. It got worse for me on the streets. It always does, my friend.

March 3, 2007 - Women's Shelter - in Waltham - Bristol Lodge

Well this is my New "Journal" - Notebook. Unlike My last ONE.. I will write in order. Not all over the Place. i feel more in control w/ my Life even though i'm stayin @ A Women's Shelter in Waltham. i have gone through alot in the past few weeks but I'm still standin.. Sober & all.

I had a few mess ups.. Well In my eyes they were. This week i was @ my moms cuz i did her hair & in my room i had 3 suboxons. So me and jim talked about it & took 1 1/2 each. Then i realized I liked the way they made me feel. I came here to Bristol lodge that same nite. i remember being on the phone & straight Nodin' so it took like 3 days 4 the effects to leave. So last Nite we* *were @ Jim's brothers & were stayin the nite & i had a physical & mental urge to get more.. But i didn't want to get high w/ oxy's. i just wanted suboxone. & i told jim. I cried & then we got 2 each.*

So now 2day i talked w/ jim & told him i feel like i need to work more on my recovery.. just by goin to seperate meetings & stra Start to Really work the program cuz im scared Not to.. i know it's hard work but i'm So WoRRied i won't do this "Recovery" good enough & then i'll Relapse.. I mean i allReady want SuboxoNE* like.. i don't want to catch a habit on suboxone. No fuckin way. i mean I've gotten some women's phone #'s at meetings But I'm Not Ready to call them.. i just don't know what i'd say.

i'm goin on monday to IOP.. So that's good. i guess i just know that what i did w/ the Suboxone wasn't Really Right even though They are "legal". I know in my heart that i abused them. So i should be scared.. I don't want to throw away My 36 days.. But feel like i gotta get it under control. I mean yeah i feel good right now.. Cuz it's still in my system.. But lets see How tough i am in a few Days.. lets Hope i can get through any urges & cravings. I will pray. & i will Remember to not become complacent & always Remember The Desperation i have.. Always do the next Right Thing 4 My Recovery.. :)

Peace & Love.. Jazz. xo

*Suboxone = is a prescribed medication that opioid addicts can take to reduce cravings, withdrawal symptoms. It also acts like a blocker. Therefore, if you take it and then try to get high you will not succeed. This medication is sold on the streets.

*Straight nodin' = is a street term to describe the effects of opioids such as, heroin and pain pills.

December 24, 2015

Denial

That's the one word to say about that entry.

One of the definitions of denial in the Merriam-Webster dictionary states that it is, "a psychological defense

mechanism in which confrontation with a personal problem or with reality is avoided by denying the existence of the problem or reality."

That was exactly what I was doing—denying that I had already relapsed by taking the Suboxone, which I was buying on the street. Even if it was prescribed by a doctor and I abused it, that would still count as a relapse. Suboxone is one way to treat an opioid addiction. Opioids are the class of drugs that include heroin or painkiller medications like Oxycontin. Suboxone is basically a synthetic opioid that goes to the pain and pleasure receptors in the brain.

When I first starting taking it, I would get the euphoric feeling of being high. That's why I liked it. However, it also acts as a blocker, which means if I took a Suboxone early in the day and then did an Oxycontin later, I would not get high. It could put me into full withdrawal, which results in being dope sick.

Right now, I feel nauseous just thinking about the feeling of withdrawal.

Needless to say, Suboxone did not work for me. It was just a way to medicate myself and justify the wrong I was doing. I wasn't keeping my recovery upfront and honest. I see this very clearly now. I see it as a trap that prolongs true freedom from drug addiction. It is like putting a band-aid over a gaping wound.

My journal cover, as it would look later.

March 5, 2007

another day iN Paradise.. (As Zoe says)! 2day i went to the Noontime @ 5 Magazine St.. it was good but we (Jim & i) left early. We were tired. & falling asleep. We went to the Cambridge Libary too. I'm gonna get a card 2morrow. So everythings going as good as it can..

I went 2 church on Sunday.. We meet Patti (Jim knows her from Charlestown) The church is Assembly of Christians. It's Born again Christians' & it was great. We felt so good there..It was very uplifting & moving. I cried & felt good - like i actually belonged. Then to my grandmothers w/ Jim 4 Dinner.

Jim & i have talked about us.. We decied that our Recovery has to come 1. meaning we must do things seperate & Really work our shit. i want to be better & i Really like Jim. i want it to work w/ him. but i want to see him do good. He needs to do the necasary things for his Recovery & sometimes i just feel like he doesn't or not doesn't want to but maybe doesn't know how. Since he's lived such a cRazy life 4 so long. I hope & pray he makes changes. Cuz i'm really getting to like him. i Really am.

& 4 once in my life i'm aware of Self. & have such a mature mind. i feel good about myself. my direction & purpose in Life. I know i have more work to do, but I'm aware.. That's huge. Plus i'm Sober. Another big Step in the Right direction.. I have 38 days Sober.. Good stuff. I had a little run in w/ Suboxone but I don't want to mess up all the work i've Done to get clean.. I don't want to Repeat this fuckin process.. Detox, SOAP. Homeless, Due to Discharge! To a Shelter.. Waiting 4 a Half-Way house.. This shit is crazy. The suboxone is a little cheat cuz it makes me feel good. so i'm not sure if it's a good idea.. I should talk to a Doctor about it. But 4 now I'm doin the next Right thing 4 my Recovery.. Stay Strong. Peace & Love. Jazz

December 29, 2015

Finding God

I can still remember the spiritual experience I had at that church, even though it was over eight years ago. It was unlike anything I had experienced. I was raised in the Catholic faith and never really experienced God in a real way. At church that day, the Holy Spirit was moving and present. Also, I was open and willing to receive the love God had for me.

After service, Patti and her friends were taking me to the train station, but before we left the parking lot, there was a divine intervention. In the backseat of her car, I wept, cried and prayed with three faithful and wise women. They were telling me how much Jesus loved me—no matter what I'd done in the past. They told me He was waiting for me to come to Him, to be forgiven and be cleansed of all my sin. I couldn't believe that this Jesus, a holy God, could love me. I felt so dirty and stained with sin. I mean, I had been a prostitute and was in early drug recovery.

I still believed the lies that my trafficker had drilled into my mind. Things like, no one will ever love me because I was a dirty prostitute, and "God doesn't like ugly." Yes, I felt non-redeemable, as if I was going to hell in a hand basket because I was the worst there was. But God met me where I was—in the backseat of a car—broken but willing and needing him.

As I reflect, I can clearly see just how good God is. He didn't, and still doesn't, wait until we have it all together and are perfect. Rather, He waits patiently until we are ready to receive and then He swoops in—gently and lovingly, like only a perfect Savior can. A couple weeks later, Patti gave me a Bible, and I began learning about Jesus.

Do you know Jesus? Have you had a personal experience with the living God?

If not, and you are open to it, pray and ask Him to come into your life and heart. Ask Him to forgive you for your past mistakes. He is waiting at the door of your heart and saying, "Here I am! I stand at the door and knock. If anyone hears my voice and opens the door, I will come in and eat with that person, and they with me." Revelation 3:20

"Ask and it will be given to you; seek and you will find; knock and the door will be opened to you." Matthew 7:7

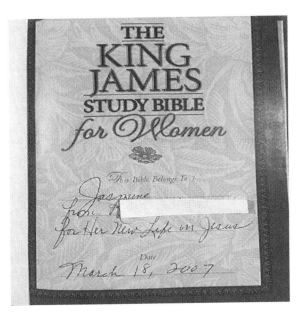

Picture of the Bible that Patti gave me.

March 8, 2007 - Woman's place -Cambridge

Well it's another day clean & sober. It's also my second day @ woman's place. I'm hanging in there.. it's not always easy when i think - this is where i live - I'm w/out communication from my family & Jim.. I get sad. But what i know 4 sure is that this is exactly where i'm supposed to be..

God has intervened in my Life because I have become open & willing 4 his help & guidance through this process. I know that throughout My whole Life, Good, Bad & UGly I'm exactly where i need to be & what i've been through has made me who I am 2day. There is nothing i can do but accept it. Which i do. even though i may not like it.. I have to accept & Respect my past & learn from it so i can move on. w/out self acceptance i have nothing. & I'm not acting like i know it all.. but i have some experience of a good life. My parents may not have raised me perfect but they did teach me some morals, values & How to Respect others.. They did all they knew How too.

What i have to learn is how to live Life as an addict. I'm an addict of many things not just drugs & alcohol..I must get Spiritually involved.. learn new behaviors.. and have more Self Respect. I need to reconnect w/ myself. Which i am.. It's just a process. I need some copping Skills..

I need to get back to me - before that terrible Relationship Destroyed me.. I was Someone. I had some good Direction & motivation to Live Life.. I was just a young girl That was partying & goin to clubs letting guys treat me However they wanted.. Cuz i felt accepted by them. I let them take & take from me.. Use me.. Ever since i can remember i let men take from me & never got much back in return.. B was no different. plus he Trained me or taught me a Hole nother Life.. He touched on the material addict w/in me.. He showed me How to use my Body & looks as a tool, to get money from men - perfect Strangers.. I'm not Sure if i was manipulating These Tricks.. Cuz i know that i never promised them nothing i could not offer.. but i did lie to them & tell them stories.. never did i tell them i had a pimp & Hated my Life.. I just was always up front - now that i think of it..

I've always even during my drug use never wanted to hurt anyone else. I put myself in horrible Debt & Danger each time. I just became good at Living two Lives.. never Letting anyone know the true me.. also cuz either I'm afraid of me.. OR I just never got to find out who that was.. Which i will by this process. Which i need to always remember this time in this House will help me discover who i am & what some of my purpose is in this world..

God by my side & helping me in my direction. Peace & Love. Jazz

December 31, 2015

Acceptance

I believe that acceptance is a vital part of early recovery. It is probably the foundation upon which all of my recovery has been built. I can thank Alcoholics Anonymous for that!

Living in a women's halfway house was hard because I couldn't get high, and I couldn't sit with my sober self! Most

often, I couldn't sleep. When I did, I would have nightmares. I couldn't connect with the other women because I felt different.

I never thought anyone else was a prostitute like me. This can be a problem for trafficking victims who enter substance abuse programs. In these programs that are solely designed for addiction recovery, no one talks about the past trauma around sexual exploitation. Therefore, women with a history of sexual abuse, exploitation, trafficking or prostitution can become filled with more and more shame. They may stay in the cycle of addiction because they aren't able to address the root causes of their pain and drug use.

Because I really wanted to get well, I was putting in effort and was slowly coming to terms with my past and current situation. I didn't stay in that program long, but I remember reading and finishing a really good book, *The Road Less Traveled* by Dr. Scott Peck. I say finishing because that was a big deal! The book opened my eyes and helped me learn a lot about myself and recovery. I highlighted the crap out of it and still have it on my bookshelf.

Back to the word "acceptance": It is a choice, as well as a process. We can either make it an enjoyable journey or continue in our suffering. Embracing myself—warts and all—has made me a more hopeful person. I have learned to be OK with who I am today and where I've been. I am now able to share my experience, strength and hope with others who struggle with addiction and prostitution because I am no longer ashamed. I have found the purpose of my life, and I love that I can openly share it with others to help them find their purpose.

The Big Book of AA states that having acceptance will help with today's problems. It tells me to focus on what needs to be changed in me, not in the world around me.

Here's to another year of more Hope and Healing!

Happy New Year to you and yours!

March 11, 2007 Sunday @ 3:30pm - Woman's Place, Cambridge

It's a day.. a day that is Well expected in these new days of Recovery.. But I'm handeling pretty OK.. I'm having a difficult time w/ Being here. Mostly cuz I'm feeling alone. & When i first checked in Melanie asked me a question that got me thinking.. She asked if i was a chronic relapser & I said no - just once - not chronic & she said than "why are you here" & i said cuz "they told me to come here"

I was @ that time in new Hope just going through so much & Desperitly wanted to stay clean so i was up 4 everything. & or anything. my Counseler mentioned "Woman's place" in Cambridge - me not knowing anything said yeah, whatever! Than got Discharged unexpectdly.. - stayed Sober went to Zoe's We went to Bristol lodge.. & was doing the Best i could w/ what i had.. I didn't know what a halfway house even was all about. But i wasn't going home to my moms cuz i felt like it was too soon & i didn't want to fall back into any old behaviors or start to manipulate. I didn't feel strong enough.. - so i made it hard.. I humbled Myself & got into here.

Came in & have felt compelled by feelings that I'm in the wrong place.. not cuz of the Rules.. But just cuz i got placed & moved through the System. I felt alone in here.. & last night i saw Jim @ the meeting which is good to see him.. so good actually. He asked me what was wrong & i said nothing & then Broke down.. not really knowing But just felt so emontional & kinda alone.. So I then asked Kim (my roomate) How she felt & She told me she hated it here.. I then 2day went to the morning meeting & to my surprise saw Zoe.. I almost cried.. We talked & I told her what was going on.. She told me She talked to Jim this morning..I cried & told her i was tired.. Just so tired.. She got it.

We talked about my options. Sober House. My moms. She than gave me a letter & left. I called my dad & told him what was going on.. & not to bring anything here. just yet. I'm not being impulsive, cuz I'm waiting it out & talking..

So i got "lucky" cuz there was Carol here 2day. She is under the Director.. I didn't think anyone would be here till Monday.. So i asked if we could talk.. I sat down & had tears behind my eyes my voice was cracking.. I told her Sorry i'll probally Cry.. She said thats ok. i told her some of my story.. & she proceeded to tell me "I don't know if this is where you should be.. But i think it's good for you & It may be where you need to be.. noone but you put yourself here.. you didn't have to" She basically wasn't gonna tell me "no you don't need to be here" Why would She.. So i listened to her & said ThanKs. & left her office feeling more confused went to my room wanted to write but had to take a second & i napped.. woke up met Sarah's parents.. had cake & begin to write..

I'm still feeling like i need to talk to someone & the woman that's in charge is Jan & She seems really cool. We get along.. I feel real comfortable w/ her.. I might talk to her.. But am i just looking 4 someone to tell me what i want to hear? am i looking 4 an answer? When all i have to do is sit back & let God help me.. He will give me the guidance i need.

I know what i feel. & i know that it's what your gut says not your mind.. My mind is impulsive.. My mind is what has gotten me here.. Cuz i stopped listening to my heart when i used.. When i came out of that shit w/B - I didn't want to feel. The therapist @ Victims of Violence was - Real - Real shit & Drugs took me out of those feelings. Rocky died (my dog) & i said. 4get this.. I'm not coping I don't know How & They (drugs) took all the pain away.

I've been through so much these past few months.. I've learned.. & learned. I'm so open & willing. I've found my higher Power & have been feeling unstoppable w/ my recovery.. I've Listened @ meetings & not everyone has gone to a halfway House.. Going to a House isn't on the Twelve Steps oR Traditions.. It just serves as a tool for in my opinion - women here anyway.. Cuz This is what i've experienced.. woman that cannot stay sober on there own.. Chronic relapsers.. woman that have been in jail - through Detox ten hundred times.. - last options.. Have children.. Bla Bla. most haven't worked in years. Have no skills. - not that I'm any better or "Different' as Jim told me last night.. "Jazz we Are no better or Different - we just have different values & morals." which is so true & He helped me to not feel like i am being snobish or anything.

But am going through exactly what i'm supposed to be going to.. & wheather i leave here or not. I will continue to pray & ask God to help me in this decision.. I'm talking about it w/ people. & not being impulsive. I'm feeling all these feelings & not wanting to use over them.. not @ all.

Also as I'm sitting here.. The girl Jan (I like) we were talking & she told me about her being sober 4 3 years has a 1 1/2 year old & needs to go to a meeting. I asked her is she had a sponser..Bla Bla.. She said no.. never did I.. But she's been in safety ever Since.. This is her first time on her own. funny that she feels like she needs a meeting.. & went to the Book Store & got a daily meditation Book. I asked Her why don't you have a sponser.. She said probally cuz I'm afraid well - actually She said - it's the fear of asking someone.. & then said plus I'm really not a phone person.. But if i ever need to I call my friend who is in Recovery. & my mom. She's in Recovery too. -

I told her how i felt & it was that I'm not saying you ever will but god forbid you relapse just cuz your afraid to talk to a woman.. I told her How scared i was. But did it. & would feel Bad if later in life her kid was 5 years old - like some of these women & she ended up back here cuz she never got a sponsor. She Listened & i didn't want to go Deep & act like i knew it all.. I just got a good feeling by trying to help her & talk..

It helped me to realize that this program (AA) (NA) & working it all the way not just half or some or a little. Is my only chance 4 Recovery.. Spirtually & Mentally.. This house will teach me How to be Responsible.. - I know how to be that. I want to be that.. I want a family. I want to be a good person.. in & out. All i want is a good Life. I know How to get it. It's my money addiction That is possibly in My way. - Cuz I'm scared of not being able to live "normally" But Same as Drugs. I'll pray 4 God to help me w/ that.. & Hopefully he will show me The Way..

I want to get The individual counseling i need. I want to stay sober. How's all the facts I know - people get out of the Halfway House been clean 4 9 months & than - BAM - Get HIGH -Relapse! Cuz guess what they had no sponsor.. Or they did but didn't utilize them correctly. They didn't do the steps.. Or they did But not in Order. They still wanted to do it some, sort of there own way.. Rather than taking the Back Seat & Letting God take over..

I have completely Gave my Drug addiction up.. I know i cannot DO it ever again.. My pain was great enough.. I'm done. it's over. And today I'm OK w/ that.. I'll be honest @ first it was Difficult 4 Me.. But as the days go on.. & my experiance's grow - I'm done. Spent. Tired. Though - even the Suboxone insident Broke me Down - but i learned.. I've moved on & last night someone called Jim & asked him - He told them no thanks.. I didn't even want to. even being in this unstabble state. I didn't want to.. using or abusing prescription Drugs is not an option. Not @ all. & God helps me to stay strong & give me the courge i need to get through this. Cuz i ask him to help me by praying..

I'm grateful. I'll end 4 now.. Cuz I'm sitting here & i'm sweating.. also feeling Like i want to call my mom - pack my bags & be out. But something is telling me to hold on.. maybe it's the fear. feeling unsure of the unknown or that I'm talking myself into leaving.. I need some more time & will go pray.. Relax 4 a second & take some time out. Peace & Love, Jazz

P.S. I wish i could call Jimmy! <3 - Plus i'm noticing myself really getting into everything I'm analyzing the girls & could Make them umcomfortable wheter it's cuz i'm super sensitive Right now.. oR just trying to take my mind off myself.. ? - OR just being aware. Do i like to help people? - or do i try to to much? questions Questions.

6pm. Wow. hours went by & i feel like i've only been sitting here 4 a few minutes. OR half hour. I feel way better then i did.. Thank-you.

January 5, 2016

Not Alone

That was some serious reflection! This long journal entry doesn't need much of an explanation today. But I am grateful for everything that I was processing and that I had a notebook and pen to record it all.

I hope this entry brings you some comfort. I want you to know that you are not alone in your struggle. Countless others have survived what we have gone through and what you might be experiencing today. I wish I could be there to give you a hug or just listen. Feel free to contact me if this has touched you.

I have learned that the people in our lives *will* fail us. I also know that He never fails us, and He never will. He can't because He is God! His love is never ending. His presence is always with us. We just have to seek him by praying. Talk to Him like He is a friend. He loves to hear from us.

But there I was, struggling to stay in treatment. I was confused because I didn't realize that I was a victim of sex trafficking. I knew I felt different, but I didn't understand why. I am grateful for the public awareness and work related to sex trafficking that has been done during the past 20 years. To all of those who work endlessly to make this a world where girls aren't for sale, I applaud you.

Thanks for fighting for her—and for the girl I used to be.

March 21, 2007. 10:11am

Hi.. it's Me again.. it's weds morning. & I'm finished getting dressed. I have an interview @ Supercuts today @ 2pm! On friday i missed My Doc appt so while i was in Central Sq Cambridge i decied to go try out Supercuts & see if they were hiring. & i ended up talking w/ the lady (manager) & she seemed to Like me.. i then got a call @ home before i even came got there. it was a District Manager asking me to come in on Weds! to talk about training! I'm So excited. I'm happy. to finally get a move on.. I even asked Sherry @ NA central Sq to be my sponsor. I call her every day to check in but haven't really got to connect w/ her yet.

My relationship w/ my Mom & Dad are changing. 4 the better. Me & my Mom had a good talk last night & she told me i should go back to school 4 Substance abuse cuz i'm really good - real easy to talk to. That made me feel good 4 her to say that. I'm glad we can talk.. & i actually would Like to do that. I just Might -

& it's Like I'm going to Supercuts - Just like when i was 19. my life - my world completly changed - & i was - GONE - 4 a while - Like 6 years! So now I'm back - w/ my knowledge & experience! I can start back @ a salon - not Great but Super! & Maybe go back to school - Substance Abuse Counseling was my First Major!! Plus i like to write maybe i can get involved w/ some sort of writting

thing.. And i want to go back to Dance! i want to go to Dancing school - So Bad!

My first thing is to Stay Sober!!

yesterday I went to the Doc's w/ non Ellie & Dad. Non El has a small but cancerious tumor in her breast. So my first reaction when the reality set in - was of fuck this - I'm gettin high. i can't deal. then i thought - no way i can't do that. & Miss out on being w/ her through this process.. i went to a meeting & talked about it.. I still went & took a suboxone, which was stupid but i did.. i gotta stop abusing them - every once & a while. Cuz I'm afraid of a Relapse. & i don't want to go backword. I only want to Move ahead.

Please GOD help me w/ the peace w/in. Grant me the strength to get by the obessive thoughts - that ONE last time! NO NO NO.... i cannot fuck w/ fate.. I cannot Beat the Devil. Please Help. Jazz. Peace & love.

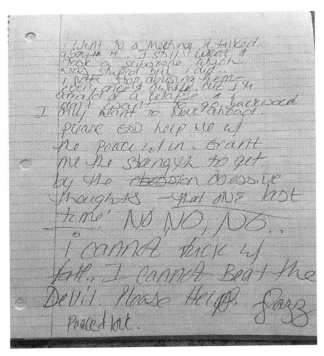

Page from my diary entry.

190

January 7, 2016

Blessings

As I look back today, I am in awe. Recovery has given me many gifts. I just love how the desires of my heart have been answered. These blessings have been given in such a magnificent manner—much better than I could have ever imagined. Thanks to God. He redeems people so beautifully.

Now I get to write and self-publish this book, and I get to work with women every week! That is one of the favorite aspects of my work. I enjoy leading a support group at a women's halfway house and helping the women. I listen to their stories and current struggles. When I can, I offer hope. If I can make it in recovery, so can they.

For the past two years, I danced for the amazing productions that my church does every Christmas. This year, my son performed with me. It was so special and sweet to express my worship to God in this very honoring way.

If you read the last entry, you will remember that I was struggling to stay in the halfway house. By the time of this entry, I had left that program. But still, I was trying to do the next right thing by getting a job. Now I can see that I was rushing. I was feeling internal pressure to get my life together. Maybe you can relate? I felt like I had wasted six years. The reality is that those years were stolen from me. Being trafficked and then living day to day in "normal" life isn't an easy adjustment, especially when I had a growing drug addiction. I didn't realize it at the time, but I had already relapsed by abusing the Suboxone. A full blown relapse and disaster was in the making.

(Circa April 2007)

Well it's me. I thought i'd write Cuz i've been home 4 about 2 weeks.. it's going well & I got a job @ Super Cuts in Central Sq. Cambridge. i get my 60 Day Chip tonite in Revere. & Chris is giving it to me. i can't believe , Sorry - had to change pens - & this one sux 2!! Here we go - Much better! Me & Chris speak - & I can't believe it but he's doing pretty good. Hes got a sponsor & everything. I'm not Mad @ him Cuz i know that he was INSANE! @ the time everything was going down.. & @ this moment i'm feeling Like getting high.. like One More time - Cuz i'm Bored i think. I'm just Home 2day. I didn't go to My noontime. & i helped out this kids Rob by giving him Detox #'s earlier.. & i know it's useless. it's stupid.. WHat's the point? Maybe I'll get a suboxone. just to take the thought away & stay safe. Cuz i don't want to go there. I really don't.

life is been good 2 Me.. I'm goin every day to meetings. I got a sponsor.. & a JOB! I think i've just been in My head alot today. Thinking of Mikey and Dave.. the lifestyle i used to live.. & it's getting to me alittle bit.

So i'm gonna shower & Read a Book. either that or My Bible..

Magine that i got a Bible! & go 2 church! i LOVE it.

Peace & Love.

Keep ME strong. - Jazz. xo

January 13, 2016

Surrender

Trying to fix my bad feelings by using drugs to feel good isn't a practical solution. Using a less destructive substance wasn't going to work. How was I getting my 60-day chip at a meeting when I wasn't really sober? I had one foot in and one foot out of the program. This is very common in early recovery.

I want to share some hope with you from the daily meditation book *Just for Today*. This is today's reading: "Help for addicts begins only when we are able to admit complete defeat." The reading says that we must surrender—without reservation! We surrender to win. We surrender to gain power. We stop using drugs—just for today. We accept that

we're addicts, and we can't handle drugs. We work the First Step—to win.

May 8, 2007

Well.. it's Me.. it's tuesday. & I'm @ work.. SuperCuts - central Sq. I'm lucky to still have the Job.. I missed fri, sat, Sun & Spoke w/ my manager & was Honest. told her i Relapsed & ask 4 Monday off So i could get Some Rest. Rather than go to Detox for 5-6 days.. I told My parents.. They Didn't say much. & I called My sponsorthis morning.. She said She'll still be My Sponser. I went to the noontime.. & raised my hand to say that i was coming back. I also went & Dropped off some stuff 4 Jim @ Somerville Detox. I miss him & want us to get better. I can't believe the 2 weeks - Since April 20, I can't believe all that we went through.. All the Boostin*, all the Dope.. & How Much it took from Me. Mentally, Spiritualty, & phycisally..

I'm beat. I'm tired & Don't want to fight this anymore.. it was good to go to the meeting. Cuz i got some hugs from some people.. I needed the hugs! I just want to get my Life situated.. I want to get help. I'm gonna call again 4 counseling. I need it Soo bad.. I Really do. I will also continue to write my steps. Back where i left off..

i have to call my papa to see How my nonnie El is doing.. I pray 4 her.

I need to get some SelfRespect

I have to KNOW that I'm better than just being a Drug addict - junkie..

I'm a Daughter, & SMaRt woman, that is a good friend & loyal partner.. I can cut hair, crochet & love to Read Books! I'm SomeBody in this Big World..

I surrender.

I know that i'm powerless.. & i have to turn it over to God.. He Has to Drive.. Cuz i'm no good @ it. When left up to my own will... I screw it up.. I was bored when i was doing good. But it sure Beats feeling useless. & Hopeless..

i gotta get my sense of selfback.

I'm trying.

Please Help me stay

Strong.. & give me the Courage to Move on.

Love, Peace. Jazz.

*Boostin = Stealing from stores

January 14, 2016

Warriors

Recovery from substance abuse and sex trafficking is not for the faint of heart. We have to think: I'm going to, I have to, and I need to. I REALLY, really want to! But I can't. Still, *God can.*

We are warriors. Warriors need to pray and be ready for battle because healing takes time and can be painful.

I promise that if you pray and seek God, and if you sit with the emotional discomfort, in time you will experience His presence, peace and healing. The discomfort will pass.

Who better than Jesus to carry us through?

Father, I come to You right now, Lord. I praise You and thank You for all You are doing in my life. I ask forgiveness because I have tried to do it on my own for way too long. Thank You, Jesus, for paying the price for my sins with Your precious blood. There are certain areas of my life where I like to be in control. It makes me feel safe. Lord, I am tired of finding false peace and false security in things that can change in the blink of an eye. You, God, are never changing. You are the same yesterday, today and forever. Your love, O God, will never

leave me or fade away. I trust You, Jesus, with my very delicate and, oh, so damaged heart. You already know all of me, inside and out. Help me to surrender it all to YOU, in Jesus name. And the people said, AMEN!

June, 1, 2007

Well it's been awhile as usal. I've been Runnin.. jimmy & I ARe insane w/ it. getin high as soon as he got Released from jail. Now He's layed up @ the Mass General Hurtin sooo Bad cuz the back surgery.. I feel soo bad 4 him. is it's not even imaginable.. The pain the boy is in. SO Much has happend in the past month. from us getting arrested in Salem NH, to me getting cuffed & put in the Back of the cruzer cuz I got pulled over w/ a Suspended Licesnse! I owe the Registry close to 600$ Dollers!

So I've been bumin around the past Day... Cuz i'm feeling like complete Defeat. I feel like i have no energy 4 nothing.. I want to go back to working. It's the only way to get myself out of this Deep Dark Black hole I've put myself in. I have tickets & Registry shit up my ass.. & i need my caR.. I'm claiming Bankruptsy.. So i need $ for that. I quit my job.. Cuz i just felt to overwhelmed w/ it all..

I'm gettin the Bullet in my arm on July 11th. I'm hopin once that happens it will give me Some time to get my shit together cuz i won't be able to get high.. I'll go to meetings.. get a parttime job & go back to school.. i don't want to go to a program 4 6 months. i'd rather get the pellet get some money & maybe move into a sober house. I need to get a Life! & I Really like Jim. I do but i can't let him Drain all my energy.. We have to be get better..OR i don't know what will happen. probally Death. & today i did get high. I asked My mom 4 money 40$ to get Suboxones & Then called Flaco.. I missed a little so i didn't get the "high" i was expecting & wanting SO Badly..

I'm gonna get up tomorrow & call Zoe get $ for a Room & put an ad up.. get some money & feel a little Better about myself!! Really i need to..

Peace & love. Jazz. xoxo

January 19, 2016

A Better Way

I remember being so wrapped up in active addiction that I visited Jimmy in the hospital with a needle full of heroin. He was already receiving narcotics because of the back surgery, but it wasn't enough. As he was laid up in the hospital, I was out hustling tricks. My thinking was distorted.

When we got arrested for boosting from stores, I knew we needed to move on to a better way of making money. I believed that prostitution was the only way to make money and get my life back together. This was and still is a complete lie. The chase of money and the lure of drugs is a perfect climate that promises relief, but it is a storm full of disaster. I could not see a way out.

I called my hustling work a normal job. I knew that I hated what I was doing, but I fooled myself into believing that there was nothing wrong with selling myself to complete strangers to support my drug addiction. Getting high was a vicious cycle to escape reality. It caused my life to spiral out of control and into a deep, dark black hole.

The sex buyers had no idea how I got to that hopeless place. They didn't understand that I had been a victim of sex trafficking.

By that point, they could probably tell that I was completely lost in active drug addiction. The cheap, rushed dates and fresh tracks marks would have given it away.

August 10, 2007

HeRe i am @ 2 somethin in the MoRning. Had a DR's appt today @ the place where they Have the Naltrexzone pellet. it's 500$ & last 4 2 Months. But i have to be 5 Days clean Before they can put it in my aRm. So today i missed My "mental health" appt @ Salem CAB. & i got high w/jimmy. we got high yesterday as well. He is in

Bristol lodge waiting to go to a halfway house.

I'm supposed to be getting My Life back together. I'm going to Gibbs College tommorrow to speak w/ a lady about the fashion Merchandising 2 year Degree. Then Hopefuly Me & Jim can Do this. I feel like such a Dirt Bag getting high. - I Really do. my mom knows & She argued eeded w/ Me. that SucKs..

Jim & I Have little fights - Wich is stupid I just want to get My Life back I wish i could say i can beat this aDDiction - but i cannot. It's powerful & Scary. I cannot do it alone.. & about Jim. I want to be w/him but it's hard Right Know now. I have to woRRY about myself and i Realize that it's not the most Healthy Relationship to begin w/. I mean we think it is.. Plus yes I Really like him - I think he is such a good guy. He makes me laugh - He genually cares about me. But the Drugs fuck up - fuck everything up.

& We Really need to love ourselves before we can function in a Regular Relantionship - We are two addicts - saying "i love you" & How much we want to be tog together. But then the Dope comes into it & that's all we care about practically.

I just want to pray. I want a good life. & i know the only way to DO that is by not using any mood or mind altering Substances. better known as "Drugs" I have to live life on Life's terms. i want to wake up everyday & live a good Life. - Workout, eat healthy, DO Some Shopping! Not have my mother hide her pocketbook- What have i turned into? a wallet snatchin -check stealin, greddy drug addict, junkie . -

when i want to be a professional, Healthy, educated, Honest, loving & compassionate WOMAN.

I want to "Grow up" & Discover who I really am? Under all the Surface - all the pain there must be a joyess & happy person - I want to experiance "acceptance" Cuz w/ acceptance of Self Comes -

FReedom -

I want to be free from self. I want to let got of all the mishaps & difficulties.. All the trauma, Grief.. Someone please teach me How to Live w/ all the pain. Tell me How to ACCEPT what I've gone through. & How to become the JASMINE i want to be. Jasmine.

who is she? & How do i get her back?

Peace & Love - Jazzie J xoxo

January 21, 2016

My Story for His Glory

Sex trafficking had hijacked my life. My trafficker and that lifestyle turned me into someone else. There I was. Fresh out of the game after being trafficked for five years, addicted and out of control. I wasn't used to being broke and having to steal to get high. The drug addiction is what took me out and what brought me to places that I never thought I'd go. This is a common story for many domestically trafficked women and girls.

I was lost in a stormy sea of heroin addiction and shame, and I was struggling to overcome what I had been through by sticking a needle in my arm. I was looking for help. I wanted to be free. I just didn't know how or where to find it.

I wanted to become a professional, healthy, educated, honest, loving and compassionate woman. But it has taken many years in recovery to achieve that. Lord knows, I still have more growing to do, but what matters is that I have found who I am and what my purpose is. Now, I am able to use that pain for someone else's good. It blesses me that I can share my story of survival, faith and victory, so other women can know that they are not alone. If I can overcome, so can they!

Knowing that I am a daughter of God, that I am loved and accepted by Him, has made all the difference for me.

I have been given amazing grace. I get to share my story for His glory! This is true Freedom.

August 14, 2007 1:19am

another Day in Paradise.. I went to CAB Health & Recovery in Salem Today. it was a intake appt 4 individual therapy. which i desperatly need. i need to get to the bottom of my problems. & i have to uncover what ever it is that i want to Burry.

i need Recovery.

My Life isn't gettin any better. shooting Dope isn't making me love Life. It's just getting woRSE & WORSE..

I have good intentions.. i want to Stop. But what can I say?

i love the Drug.

I've gotten use to the lifestyle. I'm so low on myself that I don't seem to CARE. I have to tell myself & believe that I'm better than the Drug. I'm worth MoRE than getting High & just letting time go by..

I'm not doing anything good.

I want to be proud & on a daily Basis know that i did the Best i could & lived w/ some Dignity & Self Respect.

Getting High takes all that away.

& about Jim. I love Him. I Really do. He means alot to Me. the BaD thing is that i'm not SURE what to do. cuz Here We ARE - both of us, want to be clean but we Keep getting High. i want to be w/ Him but i also feel like we Have Co-Dependency issues. We are not Healthy People. We are Sick people that feed off each other. i just wish we could get through this part & than be together.. But i have a feeling we might have to Split. i don't want to, but i just don't Know How to Have a Healthy "NoRmal" Relationship.

I Really don't

I have SOO much going on in my head..

I have so much to live 4 -

Someone Please Show my me the way..

xoxoxo. <3 Jazz. Peace & Love

Goodnite :)

January 26, 2016

Good Intentions

If you are in active addiction or early recovery, I am positive that you can relate to this diary entry. Having good intentions to get clean and sober, but struggling with enormous life changes can be scary! Getting high always seems like the better option when you are drowning in a sea of pain. I also know that facing the pain and uncovering the hurt may seem too radical. Back then, even the thought of it would have made me buy another bag of heroin. Remember, I was high when I was writing this entry. I had the self-awareness, but accepting that I needed to stop using and doing something about it was an entirely different matter.

Maybe you don't mask your pain or try to escape reality with drugs. Maybe it's shopping, pornography, anger, co-dependent relationships or a myriad of other compulsive behaviors. I want you to know that there is a better way.

Like me, are you crying out for help? Do you know what your addiction wants you to cover up?

I didn't realize that I was a victim of sex trafficking. All I knew was that I was sick, lost and dying on the inside. Shooting heroin masked the pain, but it was killing me at the same time. I needed relief. My soul was empty. I found what I was looking for that day in the backseat of a car after I visited church and cried out to Jesus. But the power of addiction had its grip on me. And I wasn't ready to give it up just yet.

August 26, 2007 2:07am - Sunday

Well it's just another day in paridise 4 me. Trying to get clean & i have no family support - except my mother being like a gustapo w/ the suboxone. Making sure i take them.

Then i got Jimmy still getting high & when i see him or step foot in Charlestown - that's all i can think of. He knew i was trying to get clean & on Saturday - no - friday thurs I go to see him & He was high - he took ultram & he thinks cuz he gets them prescribed it's OK. But he abuses them - so then on friday morning He calls Me cuz He got Dope for someone & Kept some 4 us. So He took me Right out - Then today same thing - He scored some Dope - Got high before i got there & we finally talked a Bit about stuff. & He said i feel Like - you come Down to my level - & i can't even think of How many times I've Heard that from people - & He said it - himself.

I'm starting to believe that I have to stop getting High in order for my self esteem to come back - (Or to even get one). Then i will be SuRe I'm going down to jim's level when i'm with him. I have to stop getting High in order for therapy to work - I have to stay clean Or the Job @ H&M that i want so bad is not going to last long! I hope i get it!

I want to go to meetings - get a support system intact.

Start going to the gym!

find another sponsor!

Join another group! & get active..

& Most importently - NO BOYS! -

for once can i not have any guy in my Life. All they do is take me off course & get in my head - I take the focus off myself & pay to Much attention to - HIM- then He turns out to be a nobody - A Loser! take all of my energy & time . This year I'm 27 & it's all about me!

In a good way ofcourse! I'm done w/ Helping everyone else. I must take CARE of Me first.. Then the Rest will fall into place. I need to get myself back to a place that's comfortable. I haven't been @

ease w/ myself in a long time - over 3 years! Since i was 24 I've been Running - it's time yo grow up & Big GiRls don't Cry!!

i want to get better & Have fantstic friends & take weekend TRips - go shopping & Have lunch - not Have to lie to anyone about where i work. Have to get High before i go anywhere .. lie to my family & tell them I'm OK when i'm Really not -

Please GOD Help Me - Give Me the Strength & Courage.. Peace & Love. Jazz xo

January 28, 2016

Waiting

I have said that getting high is like a full-time job that doesn't pay. All I did was run around the streets, plotting, scheming and stealing. I was running to drugs to run away from myself! It was a vicious cycle that took tremendous effort to break. Blaming others for my active addiction and lack of recovery was not helpful, but I was sick and had sick thinking.

I could envision the life I wanted to have, but getting there would take time. I wanted instant gratification; I couldn't wait very well. I wanted everything to magically get better. Putting in the hard work sounded good, but actually doing it was difficult.

I wonder what my journey would have been like if I had found the self-esteem that I was searching for. What if I really understood that I was using drugs to numb the pain of my sex trafficking experience? What if I realized that my trafficker manipulated and coerced me into buying a fake dream? What if I looked myself in the eye and told myself that I wasn't a dirty junkie whore who could never reclaim her life?

August 28, 2007   3Somethin am

i should be sleepin... but i'm up still high from earlier. Jim & i hot high allday & we did so Cux today's Supposidly ouR last day. He beat Some Kid 4 $250. & Got away with it Cuz the Kid is a punk - not from around heRe..

i Have to Stop getting High.

I Mean - Really. it's a Must.

How is therapy Going 2 work? How is my MoM gonna Stop giving Me attitudes every night when i come HoMe?

How am i going to Keep the job I Hope to get?

How will I ever Get My Life back 2 GetHER?

A Life i So desperatly need & want.

A Life that i've never even experienced yet?!

How will i make it through School?

When will All the FeAR & lonleyness go away?

Things i want to do.

Go to meetings & ask 4 Help!

Read the Literture.

Go 2 the GYM (Start 2 feel Good. about Myself)

Which should be UNO - BReak up w/ Jimmy.,,

Make New Friends..

- Speaking of friends... I saw Kasey 2nite cuz She wanted Suboxon'es.. She can't call & say happy Bday, But when She's gonna be Sick you bet your ass she calls..

She was typical, self-centered & Distant. Cold & full of Fear & insecurities.. It hurt my feelings..

So with that - i need SOME "Girlfriends" to hang w/. Like Go to the movies, lunch. Bla Bla.. - REAL Friends. not some girls that i get High with. Cuz they are useless.

& i want to so Badly Get the trust Back w/ my Ma - I want to be friends again.. Even though she's Crazy & Hard to dealw/ Sometimes.. She's still My Mother & i just want to get along w/ Her..

I'm gettin tiRed. So I will Stop writting -

Goodnite <3

Peace & Love Jazzie xoxo

-Pray-

February 2, 2016

Hope Dealer

This diary entry is a good read for those who don't understand drug addiction and blame the addicted person for being addicted. If you have never experienced a serious drug addiction, then you have no idea what we go through. The immense amount of courage, strength and faith it takes to put down the controlling substance and face reality is no joke. In recovery we call it, "facing life on life's terms".

Do you have any idea how difficult this is when you have an unresolved trauma history? I am not making excuses for the addict, but I want you to understand that even though I was in active addiction and high while writing, I wanted to get clean. I desired a different life, but the drug had its grip on me. I was in a desperate space. I was overdosing and coming back because I received the life-saving drug Narcan. I thank God for the first responders who gave it to me.

If you are currently struggling with addiction—don't give up. I know that you may have ZERO hope. Borrow some from me, because I have enough to give these days. I have been saved from the depths of hell, and I have survived long enough to write about it! I have made many mistakes in my recovery journey, but I keep fighting the good fight. If I can do it, so can you. If you are looking for treatment, visit SAMHSA's website: www.samhsa.gov

I thank God for the beautiful and amazing girlfriends that I have in my life today. These women have loved me in such incredible ways. There's nothing better than grabbing a coffee or lunch with one of them and chatting about life. I have learned a lot about God, recovery, raising children and so much more. I can't imagine my life without them. There have been days when I wanted to give it all up. I thought that the journey was too difficult, but I've had the courage to reach out, and they've been faithful. These real friends have listened, prayed and inspired me to keep going. And for that, I am grateful.

September 4, 2007 12:27am

Well hello. it's Me again. Who eles else would it be? 2day was a tough Day. I woke up & Thought about My Life. - How unstable & wrong it is. I'm messing w/ my fate. I start My job tommorow & I've been getting high. Jimmy got arressted on Saturday. I got high on Sunday w/ Flaco. Yes He finally got me alone. Then monday - I got up some money by taking $25 out of Moms bag & then 2day woke up & cried when i Read Step one in the NA book.

I know it's a hard, long journey- But I'm so scared 2 do this - so alone- I felt like I couldn't possiby do this - How can I have a "normal" Life. It doesn't even seem possible. I want to StaRt school & get a Chance to have a good Life. - but it just seems so unappealing once i try it.

I sat @ the Registry 2day & called Flaco. - got off the train in C-town & went & got high. Today - my mom didn't even know. Jimmy called - he's @ Nashua St. i feel so bad 4 him. Kicking in jail. OnCE again - & when we spoke on saturday he said - "it's over Jazz, this is what we need baby" - & He's Right.

So what's my problem? I want to stop. SO Bad - it's Like i got to Really Really get HONEST - & fucking stop! ask 4 HELP! lord

knows. i haven't been to meetings Like i've said i've been. it's all lies, Deceit, Self- Seeking behavior that i'm so used to. But Must Stop. I should Have called Some One 2day for help. I need to Reach out. Cuz this Disease is way Stronger than Me.. & it's got me- if i don't get clean - there will be NO job - NO school - & Most of all - no Jazz..

I foresee the "future" Well the upcoming months as an oppurtunity to find out who i Really am & what My place is in this world. I'm excited to staRt a CaReer! I want to grow. I want to become the woman i'm supposed to be.. Please lord. Help. xo

February 9, 2016

Me Today

Becoming the woman I'm supposed to be is the result of everything combined—my childhood, the trafficking, the drug use and everything to this very moment. It has been part of my life process. It's my story, and I wouldn't change any of it. Now, I can see that it has shaped me and made me who I am today. I am finally OK with ME!

This sense of security comes from knowing that I am loved by God. I realize that my identity comes from what Jesus has done. His dying on the cross and forgiving me has given me the freedom to be me, perfectly imperfect. This is called grace.

Romans 5:20 states, "When the law came into the picture, sin grew and grew; but wherever sin grew and spread, God's grace was there in fuller, greater measure. No matter how much sin crept in, there was always more grace." There is more and more grace for all of our mistakes.

Using drugs had made my life unstable and unhealthy, to say the least. I was dead on the inside. Reading the words I wrote back then is not easy. To reveal this part of my life, my inner thoughts and actions that are captured in my old journal entries, can be embarrassing. But I will not let the shame of my past define me or keep me quiet any longer.

I had turned into an addicted liar and thief. Stealing $25 from my mother to buy heroin is so, so sad. But this is the reality for many suffering addicts and their families. The road of drug addiction takes us to dark and ugly places. Getting honest with myself and taking a good look in the mirror wasn't easy, but it turned out to be the best thing I have done.

Being self-aware has made all the difference in my recovery. Now, I understand that writing in my diary for all these years has paid off in tremendous ways. Processing my day-to-day life on paper has helped me keep it real with myself. It also helps me get my emotions out in a safe way. So I get to share all of these moments, mostly the ugly ones, with you. :)

If you're struggling right now, I'm hoping that my mess has made you realize how strong and brave *you* are. There is power in our personal stories. I have been called a wounded healer because I am using the pain of my past to empower and inspire others in the present. I love how my past can be used for good, especially when it's for someone else's benefit.

September 8, 2007 3Somethiningtheam.

Well what a day. what a week..

it's full of ups & Downs- Twists & tuRns. I went 2 work 2day - 10-7pm. it was a long day. Then Kasey wanted some Suboxones SO She actually called My Mother & told her that She would come & get me from woRk @ 7. (wow huh)?! So she did & before i even got outside on the phone she indicated that She got high.. Right away I was happy cuz i knew "inside" that i was coppin dope.. I got in her benz & said "whats up mama? - you Gots 2 buy 4 or 5 of these So i can go cop"... She said Ok - I had her give me $45 for 5 1/2 of them. i even called julio & he served me.. flaco was closed.. Then She wouldn't pull over so i had to hit while Driving - & It Was Right in front of her awkward "weird"*

We talked bout stuff & She mentioned that she would pay 4 me 2 get my lisence back - But i can't Drive around Charlestown.. & that she'll go to the Registry w/ me. I was totally taken back. & I'm not suRe that it's gonna happen. so i got home & jimmy called from Nashua St, while I'm tRyin to hit my 2nd Shot cuz i missed in the CaR..

jimmy's doin pretty good. He can get out if they approve of a holding or Halfway House 4 him. I'm gonna visit him 2morrow. He knew I was High. it made me feel bad..

My mom - She knew something wasn't right - i denied it. until a few mins ago. I told Her i took valuim. & cried.. I wish she would go to Al-Mon [Al-Anon/AA] & learn more abour [about] Drug addiction Cuz she seems to always fight me on it.. I know she's angry that i get high. Cuz she worries.. But we can't talk cuz it Always ends up not good..

I want 2 Get A Life. I want to get better.

Please lord God.

HELP ME!!

Peace & Love. J

xoxo

*Coppin dope = buying heroin

February 11, 2016

Mercy Trumps Judgment

One of the most prominent things about my drug addiction is that I couldn't seem to live a productive life and get high at the same time! I have seen people manage to go through life as functioning addicts, but I know that their mind, body and spirits must have been paying a high price. For me, getting high was like a really bad marriage that I couldn't get out of. I wanted to be sober, but doing the work to get there frightened me.

At the same time, the brain and body become dependent on the substance. It drives you to the drug. It's like a light switch that can't be turned off. This is a vicious cycle that many active addicts experience. You will never understand what this is like unless you have gone through it. So, this is when compassion comes in. Remember that mercy always trumps judgment. When you are approaching the sick person, your solid boundaries, gentleness and love will be better than approaching them with anger and resentment.

I would end up quitting that job and going into treatment soon after this entry. Stay tuned as we get closer to the end of this roller coaster ride—only to get on another ride for more recovery!

September 16, 2007 sunday 1 55 am.

Well just another day.. I Did the wrong thing. completly - I got high yesterday after woRk - I got paid, went to the Atm - Copped - went to Visit jimmy, & felt like a complete loser- seeing him - high- not cool -

Then today i swore i wasn't gonna get high. But i woke up not in the greatest mood - started 2 feel a little sick - then called out of work - was gonna do my moms hair cuz i figured she give me some $. But we didn't have 30 volume - So I called Flaco, told her i was going to a meeting - went to an Atm in Malden & w/drew from my account making it -$97 & change - That's Right negative - got needles - Saw flaco - got high & felt OH SO MUCH better - Still Do - But I feel like A fucking asshole - I feel like A failure.. Like I'm never gonna get this - I want to so so much - But i Have to Stay Clean in order to do it -

my Doctor @ Salem CAB - perscribed me - celexia for depression - which I'm glad. I'm Hopin it's gonna help me do this cuz i tell ya - I'm one Depressed Bitch - I know what i gotta do - But can't seem to do it - 100% It's Like i got things in place. But the Heroin gets the better of Me, & before i know it, it's in my ARM - & i feel a Rush - it talks to Me & tells Me How Much better Life is when i let him in - w/out Him I'm Miserable.

I FucKin HATE

it!!!

leave ME ALONE.

STOP Runing

MY LIFE!!

I want this to be over -

This Relationship is taking all of me -

You never give back anything

but Misery & pain -

All you do is call my Name

When I'm tryin to do the Right thing.

Take your Grip off of ME,

it's Holdin me to tight

i can barely breathe.

This ain't No Romance,

it's a fuckin NightMaRE.

you got ME so bad, I can't come back - to Reality -

Something SO ScaRy.

The thought of Life w/out You is to much to bare.

I'm goin to Miss you

The Warm, tingle feeling you give me - from head to toe.

life will be so much brighter once i get out of your Darkness.

I will be able to Make My own Decisions. No More DictAtion. Watchin My every Move..

I'll be able to grow w/out any limitions.. The SKy is the limit.

When you'Re not in it.

I'm better Then you - I'm woRth More than you make me believe..

i can DO this - it's OVeR -

February 16, 2016

Fighting for a Better Life

Can you hear the pain in my words, the bondage that I was in?

Breaking up with heroin was a long, hard process. I went into detox a few days after writing this entry. While I can't say it was my last time in a detox, I do count September 19, 2007 as my sobriety date. It was on that day that I got off the streets and changed my life for good. Recovery has been super difficult and challenging. I have made many mistakes. Because I didn't give up, I have become stronger and more self-aware.

I went into detox again in 2010 when I relapsed for a short time. That circumstance beat me up pretty badly, but I came out a better mother and a wiser woman. I realized that life was way more precious than I perceived it to be. I saw that my actions didn't just affect me anymore, but others around me. I know that struggles are part of the recovery process, and I wouldn't change any of it. Nor would I judge anyone who is going through it.

Bottom line: Getting sober and staying in recovery can be some of the most difficult things a person can do. Give yourself some credit if this is you right now. If you don't struggle with drug addiction, pray for someone who is struggling, bless them. If you're near someone who is fighting for their life, go hug them. Look them in the eyes and encourage them.

The blessings that flow from a life with Jesus are immeasurable. I am in awe on a daily basis. I can clearly see how God continues to faithfully provide for me and love me.

He does this through meeting my daily needs and caring for me through the loving people He has placed in my life.

I cherish the moments when I get God winks throughout my days. I can sense Him smiling down on me, letting me know that He is well pleased with me, His girl. He reminds me that no matter what challenges I am facing, His presence is always with me and together we can get through it. He, who is in me, is greater than he who is in the world. I know that no weapon formed against me will prosper because He is my shield and protector.

All I can do is offer my gratitude to Him, which then fills my heart with joy and propels me into service for others. I know what it's like to be sick and suffering. I was once lost, but now I am found. This book was written and my ministry is done to give Him all the glory for what He has done in my life.

September 21, 2007 Highpoint Treatment Center, Plymouth, MA

Well another day in Paradise.. I'm @ Highpoint treatment center.. Yes again - I was here in January - & it was on this journey that i met Jimmy. & a few months after that i had a needle in my aRm. So Here I am, gonna try this again. I hope & pray that the Shaddock - Hopefound womens program accepts me, cuz i really want 2 go. & I'm on the fence about goin 2 a halfway house. I know that i gotta work on Me, but I'm just afraid that a Halfway House won't give me the attention i need. & Hopefound Deals w/ women w/ PTSD & trauma issues. exactly what I'm goin through. I know that's why i use, to kill the HuRt & pain. That i feel cuz of what B did to Me.. & i feel Real guilty Like i allowed him 2 do it 2 Me. The whole low self esteem thing has got to end. & i got to get a grip on my Life & my emotions.. OR I'm just gonna stay a Junkie 4 EVA.. & i don't want to live that way - @all. i miss being "normal".

i want to enjoy life & DO something w/ myself.

& find some Happieness..

please Help me.

i'm open & willing.

<3 & peace

Jazz

February 18, 2016

HIGHPOINT

I got more than clean and sober while at Highpoint. I had a spiritual awakening. I was open and willing to kneel and cry out to God. I begged him to keep me clean and put me on the right path. One afternoon, I had enough courage to share some of my story with one of the counselors. I remember that he looked me right in the eyes and compassionately said, "No one ever has to purchase you again." I cried an ugly cry and felt so relieved. I still felt alone in my struggle, but there was hope. That counselor spoke the truth to me, and he was right. Since then, I have never once exchanged my body for drugs, shelter or money.

As my journey continued, I would self-identify as a survivor of sex trafficking, five years into recovery. The shame I was feeling due to my experience was healed through a transformation class at my church in 2012. Months later, I was visiting a group called Gathering for Hope, and there was a cute little Christian lady talking about how she goes into strip clubs and befriends the dancers. She and her team of volunteers are faithful every week and are available to help them transition out of the commercial sex trade. I couldn't believe that this church lady was speaking my language! She was talking about pimps, drugs and strip clubs. The name of her organization is Route One Ministry.

This was all too familiar because I was prostituted in the hotels on that highway. Before I knew it, I said that I had been through similar things. I would love to help young girls before they get into those situations, and so they wouldn't have to go through what I did. She paused and with great enthusiasm said, "Wow, you are amazing! You are a survivor."

I had no idea what she was talking about. I only accepted it because of the joy on her face. She proceeded to tell me about a non-profit organization in Boston called My Life My Choice. They are survivor led, and they hire women who experienced the life, so they can mentor at-risk girls. I checked them out, contacted them and got an interview! I couldn't believe they were going to hire me based on my past. I was inspired by the amazing work they do. I also got connected to the National Survivor Network and saw the great work that survivors were doing throughout the U.S.

Sex trafficked and prostituted women are everywhere in our communities. They are not being helped because of shame, lack of awareness and a hundred other reasons that I don't have time to discuss.

This is how and why I started Bags of Hope Ministries. It was a very organic process. I would be going about my day and see women on the streets. I could tell they were struggling and needed someone to let them know there was a better way.

I wanted to meet their needs in a practical way. I went to the dollar store and got reusable bags and filled them with basic hygiene items. I also wrote encouraging words and some resources on note cards. When I would notice a woman on the street, I would pull over, jump out of my minivan and give her a bag.

After I told my pastor what I was doing, he encouraged me to turn it into a ministry, so others could get involved. I thought he was crazy! Luckily, he saw something bigger than I did. Two and a half years later, we have given out over 1, 500 bags to 20 different programs in Massachusetts. There are also two new chapters beginning in Rutland, Vermont and Albany, New York. We are spreading awareness and hope. One bag at a time!

September 25, 2007 Highpoint Treatment Center, Structured Outpatient Addiction Program (SOAP)

Well I'm sittin here in SOAP - having a Real shitty day - Literly.. is it Sucks. I tried to change My insurance & it was difficult - But - May happen - I got 2 figure out what i want 2 do - But I'm still feeling shitty & Realize that it should pass. it will pass - i just Hate goin through this. I want everything now - not later. gotta learn to be patient & Hold on - live Just 4 2day & love w/ My heart - not my mind - & That "God" is love - The Decency in Me. The Good in Me - That i know How to be. I just haven't been good in awhile. & it huRts. Man - it fuckin huRts. i want So Bad to "feel". I want to Know life -

All before i was abused & used by B. All the lies all the fakeness - He Sold me everything that - wasn't - He Did sell Me fake Dreams & i almost believed him - I miss My family - Sooo Much- I miss my Grandparents w/ All ive got. I wish i knew How to figure this out. SomeHow - i wish i could.

i wish this never happened to Me. I wish i wasn't an addict. I wish I never knew How to prostitute. I wish i never stuck a needle in my aRm -

i wish i could be a better Daughter & grand daughter - I wish that i get through This -

Cuz it Sucks Soooooooo BaD. All These feelings.. All These Feelings - I'm tRying to figure Them out.

loRd, God Please Help me to figure this out -

what the fuck -

February 23, 2016

God is Love

Are you still wondering why I was struggling to experience my feelings and emotions? Having feelings is scary to someone that has been unplugged or disconnected from their bodies for a long period of time. Are you in a position where

you are working with someone like me at the time of this entry? Is your loved one still sick and suffering in the grips of a drug addiction? Maybe it's you. Can you identify or relate with a lot of my words? Are you struggling with the waiting or struggling to sit with yourself?

I have hope for you. God did help me figure it all out. He just didn't do it all in 2007. He didn't do it right at that moment like I wished He would have done it!

My recovery journey has been a long process. Along the way, I have found that love is the most powerful force in the world. It has transformed me into who I am today and who I will become in the future. I have experienced God's love through the people He has placed in my life and through circumstances He has arranged in my life. I believe that everything happens for a reason. Nothing can be a coincidence when you believe that there is a sovereign God in control.

God's very essence is love. Realizing this has changed me in profound ways. It can change you or someone you know, too.

You are loved.

September 25, 2007. Step ONe-The Disease of Addiction

How Has the self-centered paRt of my disease affected my life & the lives of those around me?

- The self centeredness comes in when I'm so active, all i can do is think about - How to & getting high - I don't care what i gotta do - Rob, cheat, Steal, Lie, Even to My family. just to get High - I don't caRe what it is - no matter How bad i know it is. MoRals? DON'T exist.. Values - act like i never had them - Knowing the Difference between Right & Wrong? - I'm doin the wrong & don't care - cuz i justify it - i just gotta get High. I don't care that i hurt my Mom - My Dad- i don't care that they worry. I don't ever want them to worry about me - But i'll continually put them second oR third. - Drugs come first @ All times No Matter what - That is pretty Selfcentered

216

& I feel Bad about it.

How Has My Disease affected me physically? Mentally?
Spirituality? Emotionally?

- Physically it has fucked up my BoDy - all my "Regular" functions
are comming back. I sweat, I Have a lump in my throat @ all
times, my Body aches - I Have an Absess on my aRm - i have
track maRks - And I'm still Detoxing so I feel sick - I can't sleep - I
can't shit Right - i can't eat Right..

-Mentally? I'm fucked - one minute i cRy- the next I sleep - then i
can laugh - plus i feel Anxiety, i feel All the thoughts come Racing
@ me - stuff about the past. what i want to do - i can't seem to
foucus all the way.. I feel Hopeless, Helpless & most of all willing
4 change cuz i can't live this way anymoRE.

-Spirtually? I don't even feel like i know mySelf. I feel like I'm
Spirtually numb Sometimes. not @ the time- But i want to Respect
myself & Respect my BoDy. That's the way that i'm gonna get to
be spirtual. Stand up 4 myself. Don't comprimise my belifs. DO the
Right thing. & live a good life. Don't HuRt anyone - Pray 4 Help

-Emontionally? That kind of goes w/ mental - But I feel like i'm @
An emontional Bottom. i cried when I had to use - I didn't want to
do it anymore. The pain was great enough - I felt Done - So tired
of Being fucked by my addiction. i had left Detox Early cuz of the
protocol - & Had to get HIgh - The Hussle was over I had noMOre
energy. I felt so used by my addiction - i hate it. I want my
emotions to not be so Drastic - just easy - not so fearful of them. i
want to be able to express my emontions - & feel OK about it.

February 25, 2016

Change

**Here's the simple definition of change, "to become different,
to make someone or something different, to become
something else."**

**Ask anyone who has tried to make a radical change in their
life, "How hard was it?" I am sure you will get varied**

responses. As you can learn from my diary entry, change sucked for me. There was nothing fun about getting clean and sober. I felt like my body was coming alive for the first time in years. Everything was turned back on. I had been disconnected from my mind, body and soul far too long.

I had been dead inside. I had been numbing the trauma from my trafficking experience with heroin and lots of other unhealthy things.

Doing the steps in early recovery was a good choice. I wanted to understand my addiction and make real progress. I was done with getting high. I needed to change in my life. I have learned that doing the work is the only way for lasting change in recovery.

Step One: We admitted we were powerless over alcohol/drugs, and that our lives had become unmanageable.

Many addicts have a hard time admitting that they can't control their substance use. After they acknowledge that they are unable to stop on their own, the recovery process can begin.

I had admitted that I needed help to start this process. I was hopeless, but willing. And that, my friend, is the key to understanding where you are in your own journey.

Have you had enough yet? Are you ready to do the hard work of recovery?

September 27, 2007

Well I'm sitting here in SOAP - Listing to SoMe guy - Not interesting. But Got to write about what's going on - again - ME - MY addict Behavior - Here I am - on My Path - & another guy - & a young one @ that. Actually came in & Slowly, smoothly, talked to Me. - & ofcourse i Like it. - it feels good - But again - I'm not gonna do this - I'm not gonna get involved - Like with Jim - i feel off my path - If i can Have friendships & no emotional ties w/ Him

(David) Then Ok. But it never works out that way. I don't want to Relapse - I want to Stay clean & do this- I'm just feeling this out. & it feels good. :)

-Sorry - He's cute, funny - that's about all i know. I still have to get to know Him. But Listen to Me. I don't need to get to know him. Cuz there ain't gonna be a Relationship!!! - It's just fun. But inside i know it's Bad. - it just feels Bad - that's probably why we like it.

We can have all Kinds of thoughts - But we don't have to act on them -

What is the difference between thoughts & actions?

A thought is a thought But an action is something else.

remember to ask about that.

March 1, 2016

Humanity

As you read this book, you see that I have been transparent in sharing my very personal story of surviving sex trafficking. And more recently, my ugly drug addiction. There have been many days when I wondered why I was doing this, telling the world my deepest darkest secrets. It feels too risky.

Then, I would say to myself, "Jazz, NO! This is what you have been called to do. Even if there is only one woman still out there, she needs to know that she is not alone in her struggle."

Having explained that, I want to talk to the men who are reading this. We need you to stand up and be courageous. Society needs you to become the protectors and defenders of children and women, not the oppressors and abusers.

We need you to teach the younger generation of boys that women and girls are not for sale but are to be respected and cherished.

We need you to sacrificially pour out your lives and love your daughters and other young girls in your life. Tell them they are smart, funny and brave.

We need you to spend time with your sons and be kind to their mommas. If you don't have a son, please consider mentoring a young man. He needs you to show him what it's like to be a real man and how to protect and nurture a female.

You have a big part to play in this horrific injustice. Make the choice NOW to be part of the solution and NOT the problem.

I also want to talk to the men who are struggling with sex addiction, to the men who cannot take captive those impure thoughts, to the men who act on sexual impulse, to the men who aren't stepping into the anti-trafficking movement because they have their own guilt and shame around this issue, to the men who have participated in the sex industry by going to strip clubs, watching pornography and purchasing sex.

I understand that you may not be aware how this sick industry harms women. But now that you know, what are you going to do with your sex addiction?

We need you to bring your sexual addictions into the light and receive healing and freedom. I want you to know that when a woman sells sex and she is on stage, on camera, or with you, and she is smiling or acting like she's enjoying it— that is because she is getting paid to look that way.

I never, not for one SECOND, enjoyed being sexually exploited. I would do anything I could to separate myself from the action. I would literally disconnect from my body, so I could survive the touch or glare of a stranger. This has damaged my mind, body and soul in profound ways.

It leaves me with some questions: Why is it that I still feel objectified by certain men? When did it become acceptable for women's bodies to be used and abused for the pleasure of men? When did women become OBJECTS rather than HUMANS?

September 29, 2007

Trigger -

cause to happen. activate, bring about, cause, elicit, generate, give Rise to. Produce. prompt provoke, set in motion, Set off. Spark. Start.

5 biggest tRiggers:

One of my triggers is feelings - past stuff that has happened, has effected Me, makes me want to kill the pain.

Being numb. When i numb out, i just use so easily. I can tuRn off very fast, & when i do that, i don't even have thoughts, i just act.

When i was active - when i saw the person i Ran w/ it always made me want to use. I'm not SuRe what it would be Like to See this peRson Clean & Sober. if i did & we were Both Sober, I'm afraid it would make me want to use.

Doing illegal things to get money. if i have to Hussel, I'll just end up using. So i can't live A Dishonest Life, it will just make me pick back up.

Being afraid of failure. When i don't keep it in the day & staRt to think About the Way of Life w/out the use of Drugs - it's Scary. So i try to stay positive & not woRRy.

March 8, 2016

Coping with Triggers

Ahhhh. Learning how to do life on life's terms!

If you are in early recovery, quickly identifying your triggers is one of the ways you can stay out of the cycle of addiction.

As you can read from my list, all of those things were absolutely true for me at that time. As my journey has continued, I have recognized new and different triggers.

I am not the same person I was back then. But I believe I will always have triggers. The difference is that I'm coping with them in a healthier way. Looking for coping skills is a key activity to learn in early recovery. I don't always do this with perfection, but I am in the process!

At the end of the day, I know that I have a choice. There is no drug controlling me and using drugs is never an option. I must be able to deal with whatever comes my way without abusing substances. There is so much freedom in that!

September 30, 2007

Denial.

How have i blamed other people 4 My behaviors? - The way i use to blame people was by blaming the person that i used to Run w/. He would go to jail & i'd still use. So then i had to take a Real look @ myself, & Realize that it was Really Me. I'm an addict & it's Not His fault, but everytime i saw Him it Made me want to get High. That wasn't fair to Him, putting the blame, even though He's the one who showed me How to do it.

How have i compared my addition w/ other's addiction? is My addiction "bad" enough if i don't compare it to anyone else's? in the past i compared my addiction cuz i was doing oxy's & not dope, so i thought it wasn't that Bad, i went to a halfway House & compared to the other women, & left. I felt like i didn't Belong - But a few months later i Relapsed. - & the Disease progressed. My addiction now is Bad enough- i feel Broken down & left w/ nothing. So i'm done comparing. & i started to identify.

Hitting bottom: Despair & isolation.

What cRisis brought me to recovery? Well it was getting bad out there. & Jim went to jail, i started doing things, that i felt Real bad about. & still getting high - Realized that i Really had to stop. - My mom was hating Me, & i couldn't stop using for the life.. So i called Highpoint & Here i Am. - As we speak!

When did i first recognize my addiction as a problem? Did i try to correct it? If so how? If not why not? I first remember it was a problem when Rocky Died - i said fuck it. I'm getting High every day. - I don't caRe. it wasn't fun anymore, it was to get through the Day. I didn't care & didn't know what it was gonna do to Me. I had no idea about this progression - & unfourtonlty it has to get Bad Before it gets better.

March 10, 2016

Transparency

Working through any recovery program takes a lot of patience and courage to see how messed up a person has become! But I wouldn't change it for anything. I am so grateful for all these years of reflection and progress in my healing journey.

The piles of old diaries have served as a way for me to look back and move forward with more clarity about where I've been and where I'm heading. It has shown me all the amazing ways that God was with me. I just didn't know it at that time. Best of all, it has helped many women realize that they are not alone in their struggles.

Being transparent and authentic isn't always easy. But every time I press into it, the world opens up in new ways. It is where we find love and mercy. Relationships grow deeper. Tears of pain become tears of healing. Our wounds may have healed, but the scars remind us that we are all broken and need a Savior to fix us. He is the One who comes for the sick and weary.

I am so glad that Jesus found and redeemed me even though I was still far off, lost and struggling to get clean and sober. That is Amazing Grace!

October 1, 2007

Daily inventory:

Do i want to be sober 2day?

if not why? Yes i totally want to be sober. There is nothing more that i want.

How have i felt overall in the past 24 hRs? up & Down cuz of Where I/m @ in SOAP Highpoint. & people won't mind there business. But overall pretty good. I wish i could talk 2 my parents. My Mom isn't talking to Me, she hung up last time..

My Goals for 2day:

to Stay here

to listen in groups

to not get carried away w/ David.

to call my Mom & Grandmothers

i feel guilty about: The Shit i put my parents through. i feel real guilty by stealing from them.

i woRRy about: where I'm Going after this.

I am afraid of: using over a guy - Again - They are my worst thing. I need to stay away.

I am angry about: How people in here perceive me & David to be Doing something & that I'm here again

I am grateful foR: My Life 2day. Glad to be here & not on the Street.

I am hurt by: not being able to have a good relationship w/ my Mom.

I am sad about: That relationship w/ my mom is non-existing @ the moment. I Miss her.

I feel happy about: being ready for Recovery. I really want it & am Happy that I know it will get better.

One thing i like about myself: is my way of wanting to help people - my compassion.

Have i worked my treatment to the best of my ability? if not why? Well yes & no - I have - But David took me away from it alittle - But we talk good stuff about Recovery also. We Are trying to help each other.

Names of people in my life today that i trust: My counsoler - & David.

March 15, 2016

Taking Time to Reflect

Sitting alone and taking time to reflect is an important habit to make during early recovery. It builds a solid foundation for long-term sobriety. I was learning all types of new things about myself because I wasn't high on drugs. I sat in that SOAP program for a few weeks after detox. My family wasn't really talking to me, so I had no one else to call. The only distraction I had was another client in the program, who happened to be of the opposite gender. Men always messed me up. Meaning, I was easily distracted and taken off my path. I would get into these short, intense relationships. My counselor told me to stop shopping in the dented-can aisle! She was right, but I was willing to settle for less, because I lacked self-confidence, self-love and identity.

Feeling wanted by a man made me feel empowered. But it was always the wrong kind of empowerment. I was either getting paid for sex or I was giving it away just to feel loved and accepted. The problem with both of these scenarios is that they're not permanent. They are a facade. The feelings and circumstances fade. Before I knew it, I somehow got myself into another predicament.

Today, I know that:

- I am more than the choices I have made.

- I am more than the problems I have created.

- I have been remade.

- I no longer carry the shame of my past.

- I am loved and loveable.

October 2, 2007

Well it seems to be getting better. Fear is faith turned inside out. i have to realize that it's all the negativity & fear that will Kill you. it stops Me from doing what i really should Do. meaning limiting Myself. You must take Risk inoRder to love life. Ofcourse there will be fear - Cuz I don't know it. You fear what you don't know But you have to have faith that it would, whatever it is, will work out. As long as I'm doing everything 4 the Right reasons - Right, meaning w/ love & good intentions. not self-seeking - then i should have faith that it will be oK. it's just that i'm afraid, scared, of what i don't know. But i have to have faith in Myself. Therefore i will. it will be OK. NO fear - just do the Right thing - never huRt anyone, always DO things w/ the Right intensions. Feel it w/ my heart. Keep my thinking out of it. - i can over THINK anything -

March 17, 2016

MIRACLE!

Well, that's it. That was the last entry in my diary. I made it through detox and the SOAP program. I was living in a sober house in Malden, MA. I was clean and sober, an answer to my grandmothers' prayers! A miracle!

I had no idea what was ahead of me. I was trying to talk myself out of all the fear, doubt and insecurities that I had. I knew that faith was the only thing I had to hold on to. People had failed me in the past. They had used me and abused me. I needed something greater than myself to return me to sanity and hold me together.

After learning about the 12 Steps and accepting a friend's invitation to church, I found a community of non-judgmental people who had unconditional love. One day at a time, I rebuilt my life.

On December 13, 2008, I gave birth to my son. I remember not wanting to leave the hospital. I had no idea how I was going to parent this little, teeny HUMAN. I mean, he didn't come with directions! He just came with a lot of extra weight and baby stuff. I was petrified, to say the least.

But God gave me what I needed: a new job as a real estate agent, my parents' home to return to, great men and women to support us and lots of grace for my mistakes.

My faith and heart grew. My son is now seven years old and an awesome kid—a little powerhouse, a lover of God. He is outspoken and great at sports. He challenges me every day to become a better person.

On February 20, 2010, I married a man with whom I was deeply in love. We struggled as two broken people do. On July 15, 2011, I gave birth to our sweet, sweet daughter. She is truly the apple of our eyes.

When I was having a C-section, the song "Don't Stop Believing," by the band Journey, was playing on the radio. As the doctor pulled her out, he said, "Wow, what a great song to be born to." He was right. It was an amazing moment.

Today, God has brought my husband and I back together after a painful divorce in 2014. I know that deep in my heart, and again through faith, I won't stop believing in the power of God to continue to redeem and restore our messy past—for His glory. He has done it so beautifully up to this point; I just have to allow Him to work it out in His timing.

Editor's Note:

Research published in the journal *Social Neuroscience* in November 2016, states that experiences related to God, faith and spiritual activity can activate the brain's pathways to the reward centers. This is similar to the way the reward centers are activated by sex, love, money, drugs, gambling and music.

In the book, *How God Changes the Brain,* by Andrew Newberg, MD and Mark Robert Waldman, the authors state that spending time thinking about a loving God increases feelings of security, compassion and love. Newberg, who is a neuroscientist, writes that thoughts about a loving God trigger activity in the anterior cingulate of the brain. At the same time, those thoughts can decrease activity in the amygdala—the area of the brain that processes emotions such as fear, anxiety, guilt and anger.

The authors also state that prayer can permanently change certain structures and functions of the brain, which in turn, can change a person's values and beliefs.

March 17, 2016

Hope for You

This is my final reflection for you, my friend.

You have to believe that no matter what has happened to you in your past, there is HOPE. God has big plans for your life, BIGGER than you can ever imagine or dare to dream. If He can take me, a former prostitute and drug addict, to where I am today; if He can turn my mess into a message; if He can bless me as a wife, mother, public speaker, advocate, mentor, writer, published author and a faithful friend—then where can He take YOU?

A day in the park with my children—
Sophia, two years old, and Cj, four years old.

Glossary

This list was adapted from the book "Roadmap to Redemption", by Rebecca Bender. She is a good friend, mentor and survivor leader.

If you have not been trafficked, please DO NOT use the following terms in conversations with victims or survivors. I don't see it as helpful, authentic or appropriate. Most likely, it will make the survivor feel uncomfortable and distant because you have NO IDEA what it is like to live through the horror of being trafficked.

Bottom bitch: The person who is appointed by the trafficker to recruit and teach other victims how to "work" and to report when violations occur. (I was the bottom, so I also had to cook, clean and take care of the house when we moved in together.)

Brand: A tattoo on a victim indicating ownership by a trafficker.

Caught a case: Went to jail for prostitution.

Choosing fee: A fee paid by girls to enter the stable.

Chose up: The act of joining a trafficker's stable.

Daddy: A term that male traffickers require his victims to call him.

Date: The appointment set to exchange sex for money.

Family: A group of victims under the control of a trafficker. The term is used in an attempt to recreate the family environment.

Gorilla (guerrilla) pimp: A violent trafficker.

Grooming: A period of time when a trafficker is dating a girl to win her trust. (My trafficker did this by purchasing gifts, telling me he loved me and spending a lot of time with me. Then he told me he wanted to start pimping. I was his "first girl".)

John, trick, sex buyer: A man purchasing sex from a prostituted woman or child.

Lot lizard: Derogatory term used for prostituted women and children at truck stops.

Kiddie track or runaway track: It means just what it sounds like it means.

Knock: Convincing a victim to go home with a trafficker before the "turning out" phase.

P.I.: Another term for pimp.

Pimp circle: Describes a situation where pimps circle around a victim to intimidate and discipline her, using verbal and physical threats and actions. For example, beating with a wire coat hanger, defecating and urinating on victims.

Quota: The amount of money a victim must give her trafficker each night. If the quota is not met, the victim may be required to work until it is met, or may be beaten or otherwise disciplined.

Reckless eyeballing: Looking at other pimps, which is considered being out of pocket.

Romeo, finesse pimp: A trafficker who uses fraud and deception to lure his victim and pretend to be her boyfriend.

Seasoning: The process of breaking a victim's spirit and gaining control over them. The tactics used are rapes, beatings, manipulation and intimidation. There is actually a manual for pimps on how to season victims.

Sister: Another term for the other females in the stable.

Square: A person who is living a normal lifestyle.

Stable: A group of victims under the control of a trafficker.

Stack: Putting money to the side, whether a girl stacks money without permission, or the trafficker is stacking money so they can make a move.

Staying in pocket, staying out of pocket: Abiding by the rules that the trafficker has given his victims. (When I was out of pocket, I would get beaten or yelled at for hours.)

The game, the life: The entire life of sex trafficking.

The track, the blade: The area in which a girl walks to try to catch a date. While outdoor tracks still exist, the majority of sex trafficking is happening inside hotel and brothels or massage parlors.

Trade up, trade down: The act of buying or selling a person for a pimp's stable.

Turn out: To be forced into prostitution; also a person newly involved in prostitution.

Wifey, wife-in-law: A term prostituted women and children are required to call the other females in the stable. I had different wifeys at different times because my trafficker was always trying to pull in new girls to work for him.

Resources

National Domestic Violence Hotline
> Please call 1-800-799-7233; TTY 1-800-787-3224; 24/7
> Confidential conversations, information and resources

National Human Trafficking Resource Center
> Please call 1-888-373-7888 for help 24/7.
> Text "HELP" or "INFO", or text 2337333.
> English, Spanish and 200 other languages
> TraffickingResourceCenter.org
> PolarisProject.org

National Safe Haven Alliance
> Please call 1-888-510-2229 for 24/7 help to give up an
> unwanted infant.
> NationalSafeHavenAlliance.org

National Sexual Assault Hotline/Rape Abuse and Incest National
Network
> Please call 1-800-656-HOPE (1-800-656-4673) for help
> 24/7.
> RAINN.org

Safelink Domestic Violence Hotline at Casa Myrna
> IN MASSACHUSETTS ONLY
> Please call 1-877-785-2020; TTY 1-877-521-2601; 24/7
> CasaMyrna.org

Substance Abuse and Mental Health Services Administration
(SAMHSA) Helpline
> Please call 1-800-662-HELP (1-800-662-4357) for
> resources and referrals 24/7.
> SAMHSA.org

U.S. Immigration and Customs Enforcement, Department of
Homeland Security
> Please call 1-866-DHS-2-ICE or 1-866-347-2423.
> Report suspected exploitation of missing children,
> report crimes, suspicious activity
> ICE.gov

Survivor-led Organizations

My Life My Choice
Youth Services
Boston, MA
617-779-2179
FightingExploitation.org

National Survivor Network
Connects survivors to build the national anti-trafficking
movement
NationalSurvivorNetwork.org

Rebecca Bender
Online programs and mentorship for survivors of sex
trafficking
rebeccabender.org
541-450-9846
info@RebeccaBender.org

Coalitions and Advocacy

Alliance to End Slavery & Trafficking (ATEST)
Coalition, advocacy organization working to end global
trafficking
EndSlaveryAndTrafficking.org

Coalition to Abolish Slavery & Trafficking (CAST LA)
Advocacy, coalition building, outreach and client services
castla.org

HEAL—Health, Education, Advocacy, Linkage
Network of health professionals who combat human
trafficking
HealTrafficking.org
HealTraffickingNow@gmail.com

Massachusetts Coalition to End Human Trafficking (MCEHT)
Network of organizations and community members who
fight human trafficking
mceht.org

RIA House—Ready.Inspire.Act.
Support, mentorship and resources for survivors in Massachusetts
info@riaHouse.org
RIAhouse.org

Christian Ministries

Abolitionist Network
Equips Christian leaders to understand and eliminate systems of human trafficking
Sarah Dunham
SDunham@egc.org
Egc.org/abolition

Amirah
Safe home for women in Massachusetts
Stephanie Clark
781-462-1758
info@AmirahBoston.org
AmirahBoston.org

Nathan Project
Help for sexual addictions for men and women
Rick and Vicki Kardos
603-682-7800
rick@NathanProject.net
NathanProject.net

Route One Ministry
Support for women exploited by the sex industry
Bonnie Gatchell
bgatchell@egc.org
LovedByRouteOne.org

Opportunity to Help

Jasmine Grace Marino is a public speaker who also raises support through the Abolitionist Network in Boston. She founded Bags of Hope to provide for the basic needs of women affected by trafficking, prostitution, addiction and homelessness in the Boston area. An outreach ministry of Emmanuel Gospel Center, Bags of Hope collaborates with other groups to collect personal-care items and distribute them along with safety resource information. When women receive Bags of Hope, they see that they are treasured and there is a better way to live. They know that help is available, and they can have hope.

If you would like to make a secure donation, please visit Emmanuel Gospel Center at EGC.org/donate. In the drop-down bar for "Purpose", select: Abolitionist Network – Bags of Hope Ministry. If you prefer to send a check, please mail it to Emmanuel Gospel Center, 2 San Juan St., Boston, MA 02118. Also, please write "Jasmine/Abnet" on the memo line.

New and full items are always needed for Bags of Hope:
> Shampoo, 12-ounces
> Conditioner, 12-ounces
> Body lotion, 12-ounces
> Toothpaste
> Toothbrushes
> Deodorant
> Feminine products
> Sanitary wipes
> Lip balm
> Hair brushes
> Hair elastics
> Nail polish
> Water bottles
> Trail mix
> Winter hats
> Gloves and scarves
> Cute socks

Thank you very much for your support!

Together, let's hand out Hope—one bag at a time.

36953721R00133

Made in the USA
Columbia, SC
27 November 2018